Iconic British Women
from History

Simon Rosati

annotated by

Hisao Kondo

Junko Kono

EIHŌSHA

表紙写真：
右上 Red Cross Cottages, Southwark, London（Octavia Hill）
　　ⒸStephen Richards.
左下 Former British Prime Minister Margaret Thatcher
　　ⒸChris Collins of the Margaret Thatcher Foundation.

Boudicca statue and Big Ben. Creative Commons. Photo by Anhad Arora.

Statue of Boudicca in Westminster, London. Creative Commons. Photo by Paul Walter.

Queen Boudicca Haranguing the Britons, painted by John Opie (died 1807) Wikimedia Commons. Public Domain.

Whitby Abbey Wikimedia Commons. Photo by Juliet 220. Whitby Abbey, a later building on the same site as Hild's monastery.

Medieval manuscript. Public domain.

Stirling Castle (close view) Wikimedia Commons. Photo by dun deagh.

Mary Wollstonecraft (1790) Wikimedia Commons. Photo by Tate Britain (Gallery).

Red Cross Cottages, Southwark, London (Octavia Hill) Creative Commons. Photo by Stephen Richards.

National Trust sign (Octavia Hill) Wikimedia Commons. Photo by Stefan Schäfer.

Preface

The main purpose of this book is to describe aspects of British society today. I have done this by choosing fifteen important, but no longer living, women. Some of them are known to everyone, like Elizabeth I and Florence Nightingale; others are generally well-known, like Boudicca and Elizabeth David; a few are hardly known at all, like Margaret Paston and Lily Parr. In any event, each of these historical figures illustrates a current issue, from war and religion through to the death penalty and modern politics.

There is clearly a feminist element in the choice of women, and no men, to illustrate the topics. A secondary aim of the book is to show that women have been prominent throughout British history. At the same time, there is now talk of intersectionality, which means the connections among gender, race, class and other social groupings. The reader will note that the great majority of the women here came from prosperous backgrounds, and one of those who did not, Ruth Ellis, was hanged. It is also noticeable that many of them had the support of their fathers in getting a good education.

Further information on all the topics discussed is widely available, from British attitudes to war and the Roman empire in the Boudicca chapter, through to party politics, taxation and the role of the state in the Margaret Thatcher chapter. There is wide scope for further research and student presentations. Research into the lives of the women discussed, and the men connected with them, would also be fruitful.

はしがき

　近年のフェミニズムの視点から書かれた女性を中心とした歴史についてのエッセイは多々あるが、本書は少し趣を異にする。そのタイトル Iconic British Women からも推測できるように、本書は時代の流れの中でそれぞれの生き様が象徴的意味を持った女性たちについてのエッセイ集である。

　現代イギリスの社会の在り方や文化に大きな影響を与えたと思われる女性15人を取りあげ、それらの女性の人生と彼女たちがイギリスの現代社会や文化に与えた意義について論じたものである。とりわけそれらの女性たちの生き方の持つ意義については現代日本に生きる私達も考えてみるべき多くの問題を含んでいる。

　本書で取りあげた15名の女性は必ずしもよく知られた歴史上の人物とは限らない。様々な背景を持つ女性たちがそれぞれの時代で興味深い生き方をし、それがその後のイギリス社会や現代世界に深く影響していることを考えさせてくれるエッセイ集である。各章では、単に歴史を描写するにとどまらず、現代社会が抱える諸課題にも焦点を当て、過去と現代の連続性とその背景にあるものについて、考えるヒントがちりばめられている。

　英文は比較的平易な語彙を用いて書かれているものの、文章にはリズムがあり達意な英文となっている。

2018年8月

　　　　　　　　　　　　　　　　　　　　　　　　　　　　　　　注解者

Contents

Chapter 1	Boudicca: Warrior Queen	1
Chapter 2	Hild: Holy Woman	6
Chapter 3	Margaret Paston: Family Woman	11
Chapter 4	Queen Elizabeth I: Virgin Queen	16
Chapter 5	Mary, Queen of Scots: Maverick Queen	21
Chapter 6	Mary Wollstonecraft: Feminist	26
Chapter 7	Florence Nightingale: Nurse	31
Chapter 8	Elizabeth Garrett Anderson: Doctor	36
Chapter 9	Octavia Hill: Philanthropist	41
Chapter 10	Gertrude Bell: Adventurer	46
Chapter 11	Marie Stopes: Sexologist	51
Chapter 12	Lily Parr: Footballer	56
Chapter 13	Elizabeth David: Food Writer	61
Chapter 14	Ruth Ellis: Murderer	66
Chapter 15	Margaret Thatcher: Prime Minister	71

Chapter 1
Boudicca: Warrior Queen

Boudicca statue and Big Ben. Creative Commons. Photo by Anhad Arora

Boudicca (c. 30 – c. 61 A.D.)[①]

The Romans invaded Britain in 43 A.D. Within a few years they had control of most of southern Britain. Britain had long had cultural and trading contacts with mainland Europe, and it seemed that people were happy to work with the powerful and successful Roman Empire. In what is now East Anglia[②] this all changed when the Roman governor adopted a policy of brutality and humiliation[③] towards the native Britons[④], particularly the aristocracy. One Roman historian, Tacitus[⑤], says that Boudicca, Queen of the Iceni, was publicly flogged. She then rose up against the Romans and burned down Camulodonum (Colchester[⑥]) and the new town of Londinium (London), killing all the inhabitants. In the end, however, her untrained forces were wiped out by the Roman army. Boudicca is popularly thought to have committed suicide. She was then largely forgotten.

Roman accounts describe Boudicca as tall, with waist length hair of a fair[⑦] or red colour, and this is how she has been portrayed in modern times. She is also popularly thought

---

① **Boudicca:**「ブーディッカ」古代ブリトン人のイケニ族（Iceni）の女王。

② **East Anglia:** イングランド東部の地方。

③ **humiliation:**「屈辱」
④ **Briton(s):** ローマ時代にイングランド南部に住んでいたケルト（Celt）系の民族。

⑤ **Tacitus:**「タキトゥス」A.D.55～120 頃のローマの歴史家。

⑥ **Colchester:** イーストアングリア地方の町。ローマ人が築いた。

⑦ **fair:**「金髪の」

to have had knife blades protruding① from the axles② of her chariot, which would cut the enemy off at the knee as she rode into battle. She is shown in such a chariot in her early twentieth century statue③ near Westminster Bridge in London.

Her Importance

Awareness of Boudicca revived in Victorian times, a time when Rome was admired, so a rebel against them might not be expected to be popular. However Victoria, not least through her name④, was seen as a queen who presided over the inevitable, righteous expansion of the British Empire⑤, bringing the benefits of civilization to ignorant Indians and Africans through military conquest. The highest military medal in Britain is still the Victoria Cross⑥. The battles of Trafalgar and Waterloo⑦ predate Victoria, but Trafalgar Square, Nelson's Column⑧ and Waterloo station all date from her reign. Military prowess⑨ was admired, and somehow the Roman military machine⑩ and the bold Celtic woman rebel against that machine could both be used as inspiration for the Victorian imperial project. We may note in passing⑪ that the Celtic name Boudicca itself means 'victorious', and also that Boudicca, a Celt, spoke something like modern Welsh, and most certainly not English.

The idea of the warrior queen can also be applied to Elizabeth I, particularly her speech at Tilbury⑫ before the English fleet set off to face and defeat the Spanish Armada⑬ in 1588, where she is reported as having declared, "I know I have the body of a weak, feeble woman; but I have the heart and stomach⑭ of a king, and of a king of England too."

The island of Britain was personified⑮ in the form of a woman as Britannia⑯ in Roman times, and she appeared on British coinage from the seventeenth century until very recently. She has usually been depicted seated on the waves, wearing a military helmet, holding a trident⑰ in her left hand, with⑱ her right hand holding a shield, which often has a Union Jack⑲ on it. This is clearly a reference to a warrior queen, particularly in a naval context. Related to this is the patriotic song *Rule, Britannia*, which started in the eighteenth century as an exhortation[①], *Rule, Britannia, Britannia, rule the waves*, but became in Victorian times a statement of fact, *Rule, Britannia, Britannia rules the waves*.

In 1982 Argentina invaded the Falkland Islands[②], a British colony in the South Atlantic. The Prime Minister Margaret Thatcher[③] presided over the successful military campaign to eject the Argentinians and restore British control. This made her hugely popular in Britain. She had already gained the nickname Iron Lady, and her resolve in a time of war (however minor) placed her in the tradition of women warriors.

Another line in *Rule Britannia* asserts that *Britons[④] never, never, never shall be slaves*. This is a large part of the appeal of Boudicca and her successors. British people may have admired the Roman Empire, but those same people were aware that Britain had been conquered, and thus admired those who fought for freedom. According to Tacitus, Boudicca said to her army before battle, "This is a woman's resolve: as for men, they may live and be slaves". Elizabeth kept Protestant England free from the oppression of Catholic Spain. Margaret Thatcher saved the British inhabitants of the Falklands from a military dictatorship. Some British people have seen membership of the EU as a form of slavery to Brussels bureaucrats. There was no threat to Britain in Victorian times, but Victoria was the inspiration for military exertion.

Boudicca herself was a fighter, a brutal one, while her successors have not been. The strong woman in a position of command, who undertakes the traditionally male role of war leader, is admired, but she may also be questioned, as Elizabeth I's reference to female physical weakness shows. These women are exceptional, even transgressive[⑤], and admired as such, but they remain exceptions.

---

① **exhortation:**「（国威）発揚」

② **Falkland Islands:**「フォークランド諸島」南アメリカ大陸沖合にあるイギリス領の島々。1982年4月イギリスとアルゼンチンの間に領有権を巡って紛争がおこったがイギリス軍が勝利した。

③ **The Prime Minister Margaret Thatcher:** Chapter 15 参照。

④ **Britons:**「イギリス人」古代史においては「ブリトン族」。P.1 の注④を参照。

⑤ **transgressive:**「限度を超えている」

********** NOTES **********

her early twentieth century statue: 1902 年、ロンドンのウェストミンスター橋のたもとに戦車に乗ったブーディッカの像が建てられた。
The battles of Trafalgar and Waterloo:「トラファルガー海戦とワーテルローの戦い」Napoleon との戦いにおいて、イギリスはトラファルガー海戦（1805 年）とワーテルローの戦い（1815 年）において勝利をおさめた。
Nelson's Column: トラファルガー海戦のときのイギリス海軍の提督 Nelson の活躍を顕彰してトラファルガー広場に建てられた柱の上の像。
Britannia: イギリスを象徴する女性の像（ブリタニア）。Britannia は古代ローマ時代には大ブリテン島の呼称であった。
trident: 先端が三つ又になった槍。ギリシャ神話の海神 Poseidon が持っていることから、制海権の象徴としても使われる。
Union Jack: イギリス国旗。Union Flag ともいう。England の St. George、Scotland の St. Andrew、Ireland の St. Patrick とそれぞれの守護聖人の十字架を重ねたもの。

Questions

A Choose the best answer to the questions.

1. **Where did Boudicca live?**
   - a Rome
   - b London
   - c East Anglia
   - d mainland Europe

2. **Who was not a real person?**
   - a Boudicca
   - b Elizabeth I
   - c Victoria
   - d Britannia

3. **What is the Victoria Cross?**
   - a a station
   - b a medal
   - c a crossroads
   - d a church

4. **What language did Boudicca speak?**
   - a a form of Welsh
   - b Latin
   - c Old English
   - d French

5. **Which leader faced no foreign threat?**
   - a Boudicca
   - b Elizabeth I
   - c Victoria
   - d Thatcher

B Write the answers to these questions.

1. Why was it quite easy for the Romans to take over southern Britain?

2. What did Boudicca look like, according to the Romans?

3. How are the names of Boudicca and Victoria similar?

4. What do British people think of when they see Britannia?

5. How is the religion of England different from that of Spain?

C Decide if the following statements are true or false.

1. The Romans behaved well in East Anglia.

2. British people imagine Boudicca on horseback.

3. Waterloo Station is named after a battle.

4. Spain attacked England in Victoria's time.

5. The British have mixed feelings about the Roman Empire.

Queen Boudicca Haranguing the Britons, painted by John Opie (died 1807)
Wikimedia Commons. Public Domain

Chapter 2

Saint Hild memorial, Whitby
Wikimedia Commons. Photo Mark A. Wilson

Hild: Holy Woman

Abbess[①] Hild (or Hilda) (c. 614 – 680)

What we know about Hild (or Hilda) derives almost entirely from information given by Bede[②](673 – 735) in his *Ecclesiastical History of the English People* (731)[③]. She was born into a noble family in Northumbria, a kingdom in what is now the north east of England and part of Scotland. Her father was the nephew of the king, Edwin, and she and Edwin were converted to Christianity at the same time.

For thirty three years she led a secular life[④]. Then, after a period in East Anglia, she took over as abbess in a monastery in Northumbria, before becoming founding abbess of Whitby, a double monastery, with women living on one side of the church and men on the other. She seems to have been a committed Christian, living a simple, poor life, with all goods in common[⑤]. She gained a reputation for wisdom, and powerful men came to consult her. Yet she also noticed the poetic talent of a shepherd boy, Caedmon[⑥], and encouraged him to become a monk (we still have some of his poetry).

At the Synod of Whitby[⑦] in 664 people met to decide on

① **Abbess:**「女子修道院長」
② **Bede:**「ベーダ・ヴェネラビリス」アングロサクソン期のイングランドの聖職者、歴史家、神学者。
③ *Ecclesiastical History of the English People*(731):「イングランド教会史」ベーダによってラテン語で書かれたイングランドにおける教会の歴史。
④ **a secular life:**「世俗の暮らし・宗教とは関係のない生活」
⑤ **with all goods in common:**「すべての物を共有して」
⑥ **Caedmon:**「カドモン」イングランド最初の詩人といわれている。
⑦ **Synod of Whitby:** 章末注を参照。

6

the correct way to determine the date of Easter. Hild supported the Irish approach, but accepted the majority opinion, which favoured the Roman way. It seems Christian unity[①] was important to her.

Her Importance

Hild had considerable daily power over men as well as women. The decision of the Synod of Whitby determined the calculation of the date of Easter that still exists today. So she was an important woman, although she only became so because she was from a noble family.

All the major world religions, from Buddhism to Christianity, are patriarchal[②]. Teaching has been determined by men, the priests have been men, and women have had a secondary, even despised, role. Eve[③] has been blamed for bringing evil into the world, for example. On the other hand, there has generally been a place for holy women. The Catholic Church has always had a monastic[④] tradition for women as well as men, with communities run by women for women. Women sometimes chose to become nuns and sometimes were pushed into it by their families (as happened with men, too), but there was a viable life[⑤] for women that did not include marriage and children. This could be within a convent[⑥], but it could also involve going out into the world as teachers or missionaries. Such women could be thinkers, or musicians, for example, and there is no shortage of women saints. Mary, the mother of Jesus, has always had a special place in Catholic worship, seeming to be almost a goddess in some ways.

Henry VIII[⑦] ended the monastic tradition after 1533, and Edward VI (r. 1547-1553)[⑧] ended the worship of Mary, who actually appears very little in the Bible. The Church of England does not create saints, either. So from then until recently women had almost no role in English Christianity.

This has changed with the improving position of women in society. Interestingly, the first women clergy[⑨] in England were Jewish. Judaism[⑩], like Christianity and Buddhism, is divided into various sects, and in 1975 Reform Judaism appointed the

---

① **Christian unity:** Hildはキリスト教が分裂することをおそれて多数に従った。

② **patriarchal:**「家父長制度の・男性による支配の」

③ **Eve:**「イヴ」聖書創世記に出てくる女性。アダムの妻。蛇に誘惑され禁断の木の実を食べる。

④ **monastic:**「修道士の」

⑤ **a viable life:**「生き方」viable =「生きることができる・うまく生きることができる」

⑥ **convent:**「（女性の）修道院・尼僧院」

⑦ **Henry VIII:** 王妃Catherine of Aragonとの離婚を巡ってカトリック教会と決別。1533年にthe Church of England（英国国教会）を設立した。

⑧ **Edward VI:** Henry VIIIの長男。母はHenry VIIIの三番目の妃Jane Seymour。

⑨ **clergy:**「聖職者」

⑩ **Judaism:**「ユダヤ教」

first woman rabbi① in Britain, Jackie Tabick. The Church of England appointed its first women priests in 1994, and its first woman bishop② in 2015. There is no possibility of the Catholic Church, conservative Jewish groups, or Islam doing the same, and the continuing Catholic stress on Mary's virginity causes considerable offence to many women. The Catholic Church remains authoritarian, and the idea that the Church belongs to its ordinary members, including women, is not accepted in Rome.

Many men and some women believe that only men should be priests. Some people abandoned the Church of England and became Catholics in protest at women clergy. Others will not go to a church with a woman priest. In general, the clergy are more progressive than the congregations③. The Anglican Church④ is relatively democratic, with a voice given to the laity⑤, and it is they who tend to argue that the truth is not democratic, and that we must follow the word of God as given in the Bible. For example, the greater inclusion⑥ of women has led to discussion of who the Church is for, and a wish for greater inclusion of gays. Conservative people point out that male homosexuality is forbidden in the Hebrew Bible (but so is eating pork and shellfish, which does not seem to bother anyone).

There are few churchgoers in England these days, so many people do not care what the various Churches do. Some do not see why any woman would want to bother with a sexist religion⑦. Among churchgoers, particularly among Catholics and stricter Protestants, many accept the older teaching regarding the lesser role of women. In between these two groups are believing Christians who also believe that women are equal to men. In finding a role in a Church which has long, if not always, denied women an equal voice, women can look back to Hild and women like her.

---

① **rabbi:**「ユダヤ教指導者」

② **bishop:**「主教」カトリックの場合「司教」となる。

③ **congregation(s):**「会衆・信徒たち」

④ **Anglican Church:** The Church of England に同じ。

⑤ **with a voice given to the laity:**「聖職者でない人にも発言権があたえられているので」with は理由を表し「～なので(その点を考えると)」などの意味。a voice =「発言権」laity =「(聖職者ではない)俗人」

⑥ **inclusion:**「包含・組み入れ」ここでは exclusion(排除)の対立概念として用いられている。

⑦ **sexist religion:** 女性の聖職者を認めない宗教をこのように表現した。

********** NOTES **********

Synod of Whitby:「ウィットビー教会会議」664 年にイングランドで開催されたキリスト教の教会会議。この当時イギリスのキリスト教にはアイルランド経由で伝わったものと、ローマ教会から伝えられたものとが存在し、イースターの期日にも違いがあった。この時の議題はイースターの期日策定に関するものであった。

Questions

A Choose the best answer to the questions.

1. How do we know about Hild?
   - a her writings
   - b Bede's writings
   - c Edwin's writings
   - d Caedmon's writings

2. Who lived at Hild's abbey?
   - a men
   - b women
   - c women and men
   - d children

3. What is not Catholic tradition for women?
   - a holiness
   - b missionary work
   - c monastic life
   - d the priesthood

4. Which group had the first women clergy in Britain?
   - a Judaism
   - b Islam
   - c The Church of England
   - d The Catholic Church

5. Why did some people leave the Church of England?
   - a gay priests
   - b women priests
   - c conservative clergy
   - d forbidden foods

B Write the answers to these questions.

1. What did the Synod of Whitby decide?

2. What was Caedmon's job as a boy?

3. Who is the most important woman saint in the Catholic Church?

4. What 3 things are mentioned as forbidden by the Hebrew Bible?

5. Which churchgoers accept traditional teaching about women?

C Decide if the following statements are true or false.

1. Hild was born into a Christian family.

2. Hild lived all her life in the north of England.

3. Buddhism gives an equal place to men and women.

4. There is not much about Mary in the Bible.

5. Religious Jews should not eat pork.

Whitby Abbey Wikimedia Commons. Photo by Juliet220.
Whitby Abbey, a later building on the same site as Hild's monastery.

Chapter 3
Margaret Paston: Family Woman

Medieval manuscript. Public domain

Margaret Paston (1423 – 1484)

　Margaret Mautby was born into a prominent family in Norfolk, in East Anglia. At the age of 18 she married John Paston, having met him only once before. The couple had seven children who lived to be adults.

　John was an ambitious man, often away on business in London, and Margaret had to maintain the family house, a large manor house① that John's father William had bought. This was not easy, as powerful people claimed it. In 1448 Margaret and family were forcibly evicted by armed men, and it took② three years to get it back. In the 1460s noblemen again claimed the Pastons' properties③ and attacked them. Margaret tried not to let violence deprive④ the family of what was theirs, while her husband, and later her son, used legal defences in London.

　We know about the Pastons⑤ because of the survival of a great many family letters, written between 1422 and 1509. 104 of these letters were from Margaret. As well as the conflicts between the Pastons and others, we can read about fami-

① **manor house:**「荘園領主の館」
② **took:**「（時間が）かかった」It takes ＋ 時間 ＋ to do =「…するのに〜かかる」
③ **properties:**「土地・地所」
④ **deprive:**「から奪う」deprive A of B =「AからBを奪う」
⑤ **the Pastons:**「パストン家の人々」パストン家の人々がやり取りした手紙などの文書は *Paston Letters* として知られており、貴重な歴史的資料となっている。

ly business①, including suitable or unsuitable marriage partners for Margaret's children. Incidentally, it seems Margaret could read but not write, something quite common in her day. So she must have dictated her letters.

Her Importance

Margaret Paston lived in times of disorder and social upheaval. The Black Death②, or plague, of the fourteenth century had reduced the population of England by nearly a half, meaning that ordinary people could command③ higher wages, and could leave their home area to do so. A breakdown in the authority of the king (Henry VI) in the 1440s and the Wars of the Roses (1455-1485)④ created uncertainty and danger, and it could be unclear who was actually in control in an area. Margaret was left alone at home to deal with⑤ the problems caused by the clash between great family ambition and people threatening violence to stop that ambition.

Margaret had to run the estates, which employed hundreds of people⑥, including seeing to repairs⑦ to houses and care of the sick⑧. She helped arrange marriages for members of the household (including her own children). She also had to try to arrange defences when under military attack, though she generally fought a losing battle, literally⑨. There is no suggestion in her letters that this was particularly unusual for a woman.

As said above, her husband John was often away in London, using the law to pursue their somewhat dubious claim to the lands of Sir John Fastolf⑩ (a real man, not the Shakespeare character⑪). It is notable that people realized the importance of the law: John was a lawyer, as was his father, and Margaret had to go to court locally in Norfolk, so she clearly knew the law. In lawless times, enforcing the law in relatively remote areas⑫ was difficult, but the courts would make judgements against the powerful.

Margaret was a family woman. She wrote to her husband, "I pray you that you will wear the ring with the image of St. Margaret that I sent you for a remembrance till you come home. You have left me such a remembrance that makes me

---

① **family business:**「家庭内の様々な出来事」
② **The Black Death:** 章末注を参照。
③ **command:**「意のままにする」
④ **the Wars of the Roses:** 章末注を参照。
⑤ **deal with:**「対処する」
⑥ **hundreds of people:**「何百人という人々」Cf. five hundred
⑦ **seeing to repairs:**「修理に気を配る」see to ~ =「~に気を配る・~に気を付ける」
⑧ **the sick:**「病気の人々」the + 形容詞 =「~の人々」
⑨ **literally:**「文字通りに」負け戦(a losing battle)によって領地や財産を失った(losing)ので、「文字通りに」と表現した。
⑩ **Sir John Fastolf:** Henry V のフランス遠征に従軍したイングランドの騎士。
⑪ **Shakespeare character:** Shakespeareの芝居 Henry VI および The Merry Wives of Windsor の中に Sir John Falstaff という陽気でほら吹きの太った騎士が登場する。Sir John Fastolf はこの Falstaff と経歴の上で類似点もあるが、偶然の一致であるとされている。
⑫ **remote area:**「へんぴな地域」

to think upon you both day and night when I would sleep."
Letter from Margaret to John, Dec. 14, 1441

The remembrance was a son, also called John, born some months later. More generally, the letters show that husband and wife depended on each other to secure the family and further their ambitions. After her husband's death in 1466, the younger John① continued the family's legal work in London. In difficult times, family could be relied upon.

John Paston's grandfather Clement (d. 1419) was a yeoman②, farming around 40 hectares, and Clement's wife may have been a bond③ woman, a kind of slave. Within three generations they were wealthy landowners, and Margaret's son John was knighted.

At school in Britain, history is often presented as a story of progress to where we are now, with increasing rights for women, and ordinary people in general. Yet we can see that Margaret was a strong, independent woman, active in a dangerous world. It seems she did everything a man did, except physical combat. She was not regarded as weak, as Victorian ladies④ often were, nor was she a housewife stuck at home, as many twentieth century middle class women were. It is a reminder that rights can be lost as well as gained.

We also imagine that most people were uneducated and illiterate, but this was not so. Violence could win, but it could also be resisted by legal means. As medieval power structures broke down, families like the Pastons were able to take advantage of⑤ the changing times. Perhaps they were selfish and greedy, but their determination and skill can only be admired.

① **younger John:**「息子のジョン」
② **yeoman:** 土地を持ち独立した自由農民。
③ **bond:**「農奴の」
④ **Victorian ladies:** ヴィクトリア朝中産階級の価値観では、女性は家庭の天使であり、か弱く優しい存在と考えられていた。
⑤ **take advantage of :**「〜を利用する」

########## **NOTES** ##########

The Black Death:「黒死病・ペスト」歴史上何回かヨーロッパを襲い、そのたびに人口の減少を引き起こすほどの夥しい死者をだした。
the Wars of the Roses:「バラ戦争」赤バラを紋章とする Lancaster 家と白バラを紋章とする York 家とが王位継承をめぐってイングランドを二分して争った。

Questions

A Choose the best answer to the questions.

1. **Why was Margaret Paston's husband often away?**
   - a   He was in prison.
   - b   He was fighting in the Wars of the Roses.
   - c   He was buying houses and land.
   - d   He was on legal business.

2. **What do we know about Margaret?**
   - a   Someone read letters to her.
   - b   She wrote letters.
   - c   She was the only family letter writer.
   - d   Someone wrote letters for her.

3. **What was the Black Death?**
   - a   disease
   - b   civil war
   - c   the king's nickname
   - d   the breakdown of law

4. **What did Margaret not do?**
   - a   use a sword
   - b   go to court
   - c   manage the family land
   - d   look after sick people

5. **How many Paston men were lawyers?**
   - a   none
   - b   one
   - c   two
   - d   three or more

B Write the answers to these questions.

1. What was Margaret's husband doing in London?

2. Why did wages go up after the Black Death?

3. What were the 15th Century civil wars called?

4. How do we know Margaret knew the law?

5. What are some examples of Margaret's strength?

C Decide if the following statements are true or false.

1. Margaret was married for about 25 years.

2. The Paston letters stopped when Margaret died.

3. Although it was an arranged marriage, Margaret loved her husband.

4. The Pastons moved up in society.

5. Arranged marriage was common.

Caister Castle, Norfolk (Paston home)
Wikimedia Commons. Photo by Paul Reynolds

Chapter 4
Queen Elizabeth I: Virgin Queen

Elizabeth Tudor (1533 – 1603, reigned 1558 – 1603)

　　Elizabeth Tudor, later Queen Elizabeth I, was the daughter of King Henry VIII and his second wife Anne Boleyn. When Elizabeth was two, her father had her mother executed for adultery[①], and Elizabeth was declared a bastard[②]. After the reign of her half-brother Edward[③], her Catholic half-sister Mary[④] became queen. During this time Elizabeth, a Protestant, was imprisoned for a year (1554 – 1555), and there were those who wanted to have her executed. So she grew up in dangerous times at court. During this time she had gained a fine education: she could speak perhaps ten languages, and write three.

　　She became queen in 1558, at the age of 25, a young woman at the head of a religiously divided kingdom. Elizabeth's experiences led her to adopt a cautious approach in religion and in foreign affairs, avoiding domestic and international conflict whenever possible. One of her sayings was *video et taceo*[⑤] – I see and say nothing. She adopted a similar approach in her personal life, encouraging male admirers but never mar-

---

① **adultery:**「不貞行為」
② **bastard:**「私生児」
③ **Edward:** Edward VI。Chapter 2 の p.7 注⑧を参照。Elizabeth とは母違いの兄妹。
④ **Mary:** Mary I。Henry VIII と Catherine of Aragon との娘。カトリック教徒で Elizabeth とは母違いの姉妹。プロテスタントへの弾圧により Bloody Mary といわれている。

⑤ ***video et taceo:***「見て黙する」ラテン語。

rying. Thus she avoided domination by any man, but never produced an heir[1]. She was the last of the Tudor line[2].

Her Importance

Elizabeth I is one of the two most famous English monarchs, along with her father Henry VIII. The Tudor period provided stability and a growing self-confidence on the European stage. It is a period many regard as a high water mark of culture[3].

Elizabeth knew how to survive in a dangerous world, a world particularly dangerous for women. Her father in effect[4] murdered her mother, and she was locked up[5] by her sister and in danger of execution herself. Throughout her reign there were plots against her. Yet she was able to survive and thrive[6] through a highly intelligent mix of caution and ruthlessness[7]. Several aspects of her reign still resonate[8] today.

Under Edward VI and Mary I there had been religious intolerance, resulting in persecution[9] and brutal execution. Elizabeth did execute religious opponents, and had a widespread, and necessary, spy network, but she also left[10] many Catholics alone if they did not cause trouble. For example, some of her favourite composers were Catholics, but they were not harassed. Forty years after her death England and Scotland descended into civil wars, which were certainly in part religious wars. Her idea of religion as a private matter still exists today, in the notion that religion is a fine thing[11] that should not affect one's daily life.

Spain, representing Catholic Europe, attacked England in 1588 with a large fleet, the Armada[12]. Against the odds[13], the Armada was defeated, and, with some help from the weather, destroyed. This left England safe from foreign attack, a strong, confident Protestant country, and one which began to assert itself around the world. Virginia[14], established in 1607, soon after Elizabeth's death, and named for her, is one example. In the following centuries England, and later Britain, continued to resist European power and ideas, not least Catholicism. Britain also created a global economic and cultural network through its empire. This remains so: suspicion of European ideas and power was one factor in Brexit①, as was a desire to trade globally.

　Elizabeth's reign included a great flowering② of culture.
5 Music has already been mentioned; there was also painting, particularly miniatures③, and architecture. Elizabeth built no new palaces, but nobles hoping to impress her built fine houses, some of which still survive, including Burghley House④, built in a northern (Protestant) style. But literature was the
10 high point. There was poetry, such as Spenser's *Faerie Queene*⑤, and, of course, drama, including Marlowe⑥ and Shakespeare⑦. Nor should we forget the Authorized Version of the Bible (1611)⑧, published after Elizabeth's death but in Elizabethan English. This led to a cultural confidence, at least
15 in literature, that has never been lost.

　Elizabeth never married. At first it was thought she would, but, when it became apparent that she never would, she became known as the Virgin Queen. In this, she could perhaps be seen as filling the gap left by the Protestant demotion⑨ of
20 the Virgin Mary⑩, a pure woman untainted⑪ by sex, and one to be venerated⑫. Alternatively, she can be seen as a strong woman who had no need of men and who successfully resisted their attempts to control her.

　She was also, perhaps, a queen bee, a powerful woman who
25 enjoyed the attention of men, and had little interest in other women. Elizabeth probably had no other option, but, in choosing not to marry, she failed in one vital aspect of any monarch's role, by not producing an heir. She was the last of the Tudors, and was followed, disastrously, by the Scottish Stu-
30 arts⑬.

---

① **Brexit:** イギリスは2016年6月23日の国民投票で欧州連合(EU)から離脱することを決定した。この決定以降、Britainとexitを組み合わせたBrexitということばが使われるようになった。
② **flowering:**「全盛期」
③ **miniature(s):**「細密画」
④ **Burghley House:**「バーリー邸」Lincolnshire州にあるエリザベス朝様式の大邸宅。
⑤ ***Faerie Queene*:**「妖精の女王」エリザベス朝を代表する詩人Edmund Spenser(1552?〜99)の代表作で、アレゴリーをふんだんに用いた長編詩。Elizabeth Iに捧げられた。
⑥ **Marlowe:** エリザベス朝の詩人・劇作家 Christopher Marlowe(1564〜93)。
⑦ **Shakespeare:** エリザベス朝の詩人・劇作家。William Shakespeare(1564〜1616)
⑧ **the Authorized Version of the Bible(1611):** James Iによって編纂された『欽定英訳聖書』。the King James Versionと呼ばれることもある。
⑨ **demotion:**「降格・地位を低くすること」
⑩ **the Virgin Mary:**「処女マリア」マリア信仰はカトリックのもの。
⑪ **untainted:**「汚されていない」
⑫ **venerate:**「神聖視し尊ぶ」
⑬ **the Scottish Stuart(s):** Stuart家は元々スコットランドの宰相兼財務長官(stewart = steward)を務める家であった。Mary (Queen of Scots)の時に綴りをStuartに変えた。

Questions

A Choose the best answer to the questions.

1. **What was the order of monarchs?**
   a Henry, Edward, Mary, Elizabeth
   b Henry, Elizabeth, Mary, Edward
   c Henry, Mary, Edward, Elizabeth
   d Henry, Elizabeth, Edward, Mary

2. **What do we learn of men in Elizabeth's life?**
   a She avoided contact with men.
   b She married but had no children.
   c She had a child outside marriage.
   d She liked men but remained independent.

3. **How can we describe Elizabeth?**
   a cautious
   b intolerant
   c stupid
   d weak

4. **Which of the arts of Elizabeth's time has had the biggest influence?**
   a music
   b painting
   c literature
   d architecture

5. **What was Elizabeth's failure?**
   a England was defeated by Spain.
   b A religious civil war started.
   c She had no heir.
   d She destroyed Catholic music.

B Write the answers to these questions.

1. What happened to Elizabeth's mother?

2. What are two examples of Elizabeth's caution?

3. What happened in the 1640s?

4. Who are three great Elizabethan writers?

5. How was Elizabeth similar to the Virgin Mary?

C Decide if the following statements are true or false.

1. Elizabeth was the third child of Henry VIII to reign.

2. Elizabeth had enemies killed.

3. Elizabeth was a music lover.

4. Spain seemed stronger than England.

5. Many English people still do not trust mainland Europeans.

Elizabeth I (The Darnley Portrait, c.1575)
Wikimedia Commons

Chapter 5
Mary, Queen of Scots: Maverick Queen

Mary Queen of Scots (after Nicholas Hilliard)
Wikimedia Commons.

Mary Stuart (1542 – 1587)

Mary Stuart became queen of Scotland when she was six days old. She spent her childhood in France and in 1558, aged 15, married the Dauphin, Francis①. When he became King of France in 1559, Mary became Queen. Francis died in 1560 and Mary returned to Scotland. She later married her cousin, Lord Darnley②. In 1567 their residence was destroyed in an explosion, and Darnley was found murdered. Three months later Mary married Earl Bothwell, who was strongly suspected of arranging Darnley's death. Two months after that she was forced to abdicate③ by a popular uprising④.

She fled to England, hoping for support from her cousin Queen Elizabeth⑤. She had, however, previously claimed the English throne, and was seen by many Catholics in the north of England as the rightful queen⑥. Elizabeth had Mary imprisoned. Finally, Mary was found guilty of plotting against Elizabeth, and was executed in 1587. She died as dramatically as she had lived, wearing the red robes of a Catholic martyr⑦.

The Catholic woman Mary was unpopular with many pow-

① **Francis:**（1544 ～ 60）フランス王フランソワⅡ世。
② **Lord Darnley:**（1545 ～ 67）後の James I の父。Mary とははとこ（再従兄）の関係にあたる。cousin＝「縁者・親類」
③ **abdicate:**「退位する」
④ **uprising:**「反乱」
⑤ **Queen Elizabeth:** Elizabeth I (1533 ～ 1603)。Mary は Elizabeth の祖父 Henry VII の娘 Margaret の孫にあたる。つまり Mary と Elizabeth とはそれぞれ Henry VII の血をひく親戚。
⑥ **the rightful queen:** Mary はカトリックであり、一方 Elizabeth はプロテスタントであった。
⑦ **martyr:**「殉教者」

erful Protestant men in Scotland. She also seems to have had very poor judgement in her choice of men. Her tumultuous life was one of intrigue, murder and adultery, and ultimately of failure. But she did have a son, James, who became king of Scotland, and later England, and continued the Stuart line.

Her Importance

Mary, Queen of Scots, is probably the best known Scottish person in history. Her title, by which she is always known, distinguishes her from her contemporary Mary I of England, but it also defines her as Scottish above all else. It is also interesting that she is Queen of Scots and not Queen of Scotland, the queen of a people rather than a place.

Scotland is not a part of England. It has always managed to remain a separate country, unlike Wales, which is a mere principality①. This remained the case following the union of the Scottish and English crowns② in 1603 under James VI & I (Mary's son), and the Act of Union of 1707③, when Scotland ceased to have its own Parliament. Scotland has its own legal and educational systems. Often UK government statistics are gathered separately for Scotland. The country now once again has its own Parliament at Holyrood in Edinburgh④, with some tax-raising powers.

England invaded Scotland on numerous occasions, inflicting heavy damage, and the Scots sometimes see themselves as innocent victims of endless English aggression and arrogance. But the Scots often invaded England, too. The famous lament *Flowers of the Forest* is for the Scottish dead at the battle of Flodden⑤, in England, in 1513, at which the Scottish king James IV was killed, along with thousands of other Scots. Scotland was invading England in support of⑥ the French, who were fighting Henry VIII of England at the time. The final invasion was in 1745 in the failed Jacobite rebellion⑦, which wanted to put the Stuarts back on the throne, in the form of the Catholic, French-speaking Bonnie Prince Charlie.

The link between Scotland and France was known as the Auld Alliance⑧, one that persisted despite religious differenc-

① **principality:**「独立した自治体」the Principality= ウェールズ
② **crown(s):**「王権」
③ **Act of Union of 1707:** Act of Union =「連合法」連合法にはイングランドとウェールズ(1536)、大ブリテンとアイルランド(1800)などがある。イングランドとスコットランドの連合法は1707年に成立した。
④ **Holyrood in Edinburgh:** スコットランドの首府エジンバラにあって、スコットランド王の居城ホーリールード宮殿のある地域。
⑤ **the battle of Flodden:** イングランド北部のFlodden Field で James IV 率いるスコットランド軍がイングランドと戦い敗れた。
⑥ **in support of:**「～を支持して」
⑦ **Jacobite rebellion:**「ジャコバイトの乱」Jacobite = 名誉革命(1688)で王位を追われた James II の支持者。Jacobite は Stuart 王家の復活をはかって、フランスに亡命していた Prince Charles (Bonny Prince Charlie) のもと反乱を起こした。
⑧ **Auld Alliance:** スコットランドとフランスとの13世紀から16世紀におよぶ古い同盟関係。Auld=old。

es after the Reformation①. It was useful for Scotland to have protection against its more powerful neighbour, as it was for France to be able to attack England on two fronts. European influence can be seen in Scottish law, which, unlike English law, is based on Roman law②, and in Scottish aristocratic architecture. In the later eighteenth century Edinburgh became one of the great centres of the Enlightenment③, considerably influenced by French thought. Many Scots did well in the worldwide British Empire. In 2016 Scotland voted by 62% to 38% to stay in the EU, a result very different from that in England and Wales.

　Mary is in some ways an unlikely symbol for Scotland. She was a strongly Catholic queen of a Protestant country, forced out only seven years after returning from France. The contrast between Mary's wild life and the steely④ self-control of Elizabeth in England is striking. Ultimately, Mary's Catholic intrigues left Elizabeth no choice but to have her executed, even though killing a queen set a dangerous precedent.

　All this is unlikely, indeed, but the Jacobite rebellions are also unlikely symbols for Scotland: attempts by Catholic Highlanders⑤ to put a French-speaking Catholic on the throne of England and Scotland. The 1745 rebellion was greeted with as much horror in Lowland Edinburgh as in London. Current symbols of Scotland such as tartan⑥ and bagpipes⑦ are also from the Highlands. No matter⑧: Mary, like the Jacobites and tartan, is Scottish, not English.

　To English people Mary can seem to represent Scottish disorder and failure, in contrast to the settled and successful rule of Elizabeth I. On the other hand, Elizabeth is a figure to respect rather than love. Mary's life seems to have a human warmth lacking in Elizabeth; she is a romantic figure. And, of course, it was her son⑨ who took the English throne after Elizabeth.

---

① **the Reformation:**「宗教改革」
② **Roman law:** 古代ローマ時代の法律。ヨーロッパの多くの国々では古代ローマの法律を基本に近代の法律が作られている。スコットランドもその例外ではないが、イングランドは独自の Common law（慣習法）を持っている。
③ **the Enlightenment:**「啓蒙運動」17〜18世紀にヨーロッパで起こった人間の理性を重視する思想運動。
④ **steely:**「（物事に）動じない・無慈悲な」
⑤ **Highlanders:** スコットランド北西部高地地方のHighland 地方の人々。Highland 地方はケルト系の人々が住みゲール（Gael）語が話されていた。
⑥ **tartan:** Highlanders が着用した格子縞の毛織物。
⑦ **bagpipes:** 皮袋の中に空気を吹き込んで演奏するスコットランドの民族楽器。
⑧ **No matter:**「かまわない・問題ではない」ここでは「何はともあれ」くらいの意味。
⑨ **her son:** James I 王権神授説を信奉し『欽定英訳聖書』を出版させる。

Questions

A Choose the best answer to the questions.

1. **How many husbands did Mary Queen of Scots have?**
   a none
   b one
   c two
   d three

2. **Why did Elizabeth I have Mary executed?**
   a Mary was Scottish.
   b Mary was Catholic.
   c Mary plotted against Elizabeth.
   d Mary was a murderer.

3. **What is Scotland?**
   a a country
   b a county
   c a principality
   d a region

4. **When was the last Scottish invasion of England?**
   a 1513
   b 1603
   c 1707
   d 1745

5. **What did not come from the Highlands of Scotland?**
   a the 1745 Jacobite rebellion
   b Enlightenment thought
   c tartan
   d bagpipes

B Write the answers to these questions.

1. Why did Elizabeth imprison Mary?

2. What was one success in Mary's life, unlike Elizabeth?

3. Why was Bonnie Prince Charlie a strange choice for king?

4. What was the Auld Alliance?

5. Why did Elizabeth hesitate to kill Mary?

C Decide if the following statements are true or false.

1. Mary was queen of two countries.

2. Mary was not related to Elizabeth.

3. England invaded Scotland in 1513.

4. Scotland has had no Parliament since 1707.

5. Unlike England, Scotland voted to stay in the EU in 2016.

Chapter 6
Mary Wollstonecraft: Feminist

Mary Wollstonecraft (1790) Wikimedia Commons. Photo by Tate Britain (Gallery)

Mary Wollstonecraft (1759 – 1797)

Mary Wollstonecraft was born in London, into a comfortable family. Unfortunately, her father wasted the family money, and Mary had to give up her inheritance. He was also violent to his wife, and the young Mary would sometimes lie outside her mother's bedroom door to prevent him from getting in.

She was an independent thinker. In 1784 her sister Eliza suffered severe depression following childbirth, and Mary persuaded her to leave her husband and baby, a highly unconventional act. She supported herself①, as a lady's companion② at first, and then by running a school. In 1787 she decided to become a professional writer, something rare for a woman; as she said, she wanted to be 'the first of a new genus③'. She wrote and published a great deal, and was well known and respected in London intellectual circles. Her most famous work, *A Vindication of the Rights of Woman*④, was published in 1792.

Wollstonecraft also had an independent approach in her

① **support(ed) herself:** 「自活する」
② **lady's companion:** 貴族の女性の付添。
③ **genus:** 「部類・類」
④ *A Vindication of the Rights of Woman:* 「女性の権利の擁護」メアリ・ウルストンクラフトによって1792年に書かれた。当時としては過激なその内容によって様々な批判を浴びた。

love life. In March 1797, pregnant, she married William Godwin, though the couple lived in adjoining houses so both could keep their independence. In August she gave birth to a daughter, Mary, but died of infection ten days later. The daughter became Mary Shelley, the writer of *Frankenstein*.

Her Importance

Mary Wollstonecraft is a powerful symbol of the feminist movement, a reminder that the struggle for equality has been a long one, with progress slow and difficult. One of the key things Wollstonecraft stressed was the importance of education to the progress of women. Her view was that if women in her time were indeed inferior to men, it was because they were not educated. It was also a reason why women relied more on feeling than intellect – their intellect was not developed.

Progress towards equal education for boys and girls has been slow, and is connected with the question of the purpose of education. Wollstonecraft advocated the rights of women, and wanted to make a living as a professional writer, an unusual thing even for a man in those days. She was therefore advocating education for the world as it should be, rather than the world as it is. To educate girls to know, to think and to question, and then expect them to be obedient wives and mothers, could only lead to disappointment, anger and bitterness. Until quite recently education for girls would include domestic science – cooking and sewing – while boys would learn woodwork. This was preparation for future roles. This is something Wollstonecraft, with her unconventional attitudes towards sex and marriage, most certainly did not accept.

Another question is whether male and female brains are different. Perhaps boys are naturally better at science and girls are naturally better at languages. Perhaps boys are more rational and girls more emotional. Wollstonecraft did not accept this either, and recent research suggests that although there are brain differences, they are only minor. They are certainly not enough to justify limiting any child's educational opportunities on gender grounds①.

　Another aspect of the question of the purpose of education involves class. Here, Wollstonecraft's ideas are less appealing. She advocated educating all children together up to the age of nine, and then separating them. The rich, and exceptional poor children, would go to one school, and the poor (most children) to another. Separate educations would prepare them for their role in life. The late eighteenth century saw the Industrial Revolution in full swing②, with great need for factory workers, who would not need very much education. British governments were long suspicious of education for the masses, in case③ they read dangerous books and got dangerous ideas. The idea that the primary purpose of education is to prepare children for employment remains strong; music and art lessons, and the humanities④ in general, are under constant pressure in the face of stress⑤ on English language, mathematics and science, for example.

　Until the 1960s secondary education in England and Wales included grammar schools⑥ and secondary modern schools. In this system, children took a test at eleven. The top children would go to grammar schools and receive an academic education before going to university, while most would go to secondary modern schools and receive a vocational⑦ education, before starting work at 16 or, now, 18. In theory grammar schools were for any able child, but in practice they were full of middle class children, with occasional bright working class ones. Parts of England, such as prosperous Kent, still retain this old, socially divisive⑧ system. It was a pet project of the Prime Minister, Theresa May⑨, to extend this system across the country, and she provided money to do so. So Wollstonecraft's ideas about educating the poor, from a rather young age, whether nine or eleven, to accept their social station⑩ still persist⑪.

---

① **on gender grounds:**「性別が理由で」ground(s) =「理由・根拠」

② **the Industrial Revolution in full swing:**「産業革命全盛期」

③ **in case:**「〜だといけないので」

④ **the humanities:**「人文科学」
⑤ **stress:**「強調」

⑥ **grammar school:** 学問のことばであったラテン語を教える学校。

⑦ **vocational:**「職業訓練の」
⑧ **divisive:**「不和や軋轢を生じさせる」
⑨ **Theresa May:** 保守党の政治家。2016年7月から歴代二人目の女性首相。
⑩ **social station:**「社会的身分」
⑪ **persist:**「（好ましくない制度、慣習が）存続する・しつこく残る」

Questions

A Choose the best answer to the questions.

1. **What can we say about Mary's childhood?**
   a Her family was always comfortable.   b Her family was always poor.
   c Her family was well off, then poor.   d Her family was poor, then rich.

2. **How many of Mary's jobs are mentioned?**
   a one   b two
   c three   d four

3. **Why did Wollstonecraft think women were inferior to men?**
   a They were naturally inferior.   b They relied on emotion.
   c They lacked education.   d They lacked money.

4. **Why are the humanities under pressure?**
   a They do not seem useful in getting jobs.   b They are boring.
   c They are politically dangerous.   d They are too difficult.

5. **At what age did Wollstonecraft want to separate children for education?**
   a at birth   b from the start of school
   c at age nine   d at age eleven

B Write the answers to these questions.

1. In what two ways was Wollstonecraft's childhood difficult?

2. How was Wollstonecraft's love life unusual for her time?

3. Why might Wollstonecraft's educational ideas be unacceptable today?

4. Who mainly goes to grammar schools?

5. Why did the government fear educated workers?

C Decide if the following statements are true or false.

1. Wollstonecraft was an only child.

2. Wollstonecraft wrote *Frankenstein*.

3. In general, Wollstonecraft supported separate education for rich and poor children.

4. Grammar school leads to university.

5. Kent probably has a lot of middle class people.

Newington Green Unitarian Church, London, attended by Wollstonecraft in the years after 1784.
Wikimedia Commons. Photo by Carbon Caryatid.

Chapter 7

Florence Nightingale: Nurse

Florence Nightingale
Wikimedia Commons. Library of Congress.

Florence Nightingale (1820 – 1910)

   Florence Nightingale was born in Florence, Italy, in 1820, into a wealthy upper-class family, and was named for the city of her birth. She grew up in Hampshire① and Derbyshire②, and was educated in languages and mathematics by her father.

   Nightingale felt a calling③ to be a nurse, an unsuitable job for a rich woman, and despite strong opposition from her mother, became one in 1844. During the Crimean War (1853 – 1856), when Britain, France and the Ottomans④ fought Russia, she became famous for her efforts to improve conditions for wounded soldiers. Following a newspaper report about her doing her hospital rounds⑤ at night, she became known as The Lady with the Lamp.

   In fact⑥ her later healthcare work was probably more important. She was also a distinguished mathematician, who used statistics in her work, but that is not widely remembered. While she had some good women friends, she generally regarded women as weak, particularly those from her own class.

   From 1857 onwards Nightingale was often ill, and some-

① **Hampshire:** イングランド南部の州。
② **Derbyshire:** イングランド中部の州。
③ **calling:**「天職」

④ **the Ottomans:**「オスマン帝国のトルコ人」p.46 注⑤参照

⑤ **rounds:**「巡回」

⑥ **In fact:**「実は」読者にとって意外に思われることを述べるときに用いる。

times bedridden①, but she continued working energetically. When she died in London in 1910, her family refused an offer of burial in Westminster Abbey②. She is buried in a village in Hampshire.

Her Importance

Florence Nightingale can be seen as an archetypal③ female figure. She was a woman behind the scenes④, a nurse, whose job was to care for men, to tend to their physical injuries and bring a little kindness into their lives. Once restored⑤ by female tender loving care, they would rejoin the male world of battle.

Nursing in Britain remains an overwhelmingly⑥ female occupation. Male nurses are often assumed to be gay, as if caring for others is not manly. Nursing is seen as a vocation⑦, and is thus a relatively low status and badly paid job. There was a TV drama about nurses in the years around 1980 called *Angels* (slightly ironically, as they behaved wildly when off duty⑧) and another from 2004-2006 called *No Angels*, and nurses are indeed seen as angels. The stereotype persists.

Rather more interesting is the change in attitude towards ordinary soldiers that Nightingale helped to bring about⑨. The ruling class in Britain felt a mixture of fear and contempt towards ordinary people, not only soldiers, to some extent regarding them as not fully human. In Napoleon's day, fifty years before the Crimean War, the Duke of Wellington⑩ referred to his own soldiers as 'the scum of the earth'. The men were expendable⑪, and it was not worth wasting money⑫ on caring for them. Nightingale's activities brought a great improvement in survival rates, which showed the military and economic benefit of caring for the men. They continued to be expendable, however, at least until the First World War, with its mass slaughter⑬.

Nightingale believed in⑭ health care for all, and regarded secular hospitals⑮ as better than religious ones. She felt that religious groups cared more about saving people's souls than saving their lives. She was keen for nursing to be a profession:

① **bedridden:**「寝たきりの」
② **Westminster Abbey:**「ウェストミンスター寺院」国王の戴冠式や葬儀が行われる由緒ある寺院。またここには歴史上重要な芸術家・科学者・政治家などが埋葬されている。
③ **archetypal:**「典型的な・手本となるべき」
④ **behind the scenes:**「舞台裏の・陰の」
⑤ **restored:**「(健康などを)回復する」
⑥ **overwhelmingly:**「圧倒的に」
⑦ **vocation:**「聖職」
⑧ **off duty:**「非番」
⑨ **bring about:**「引き起こす」
⑩ **Duke of Wellington:** ウェリントン公爵。ナポレオン戦争時のイギリス軍の将軍。ワーテルローの戦いでナポレオン軍を破った。また、ウェリントン将軍はイギリスの徴募兵のことを the scum of the earth:「世間のくずども」と述べた。
⑪ **expendable:**「使い捨ての・消耗品の」
⑫ **(be) worth ～ing:**「～する価値がある」
⑬ **mass slaughter:**「大量殺戮」
⑭ **believe in:**「～の価値を信じる」
⑮ **secular hospital(s):** 教会とは無関係な病院。

Dickens[①] has one character, Sarah Gamp, in *Martin Chuzzlewit*, who is a nurse, and also incompetent[②], negligent[③], drunk and corrupt, and it seems this was barely an exaggeration.

In the 1870s she fought for famine relief in India, pointing out that British policy made famines there worse. She also campaigned for reform of the prostitution laws, which seemed mainly designed to protect men from disease, with no regard for[④] the women. She was not alone in her campaigns. In the 1840s Mayhew[⑤] documented the lives of the London poor; Snow[⑥] demonstrated that cholera was water borne in 1854; and the Great Stink[⑦] of 1858, which affected London rich and poor alike, forced the authorities[⑧] to do something about human waste and sanitation, a major Nightingale concern. Nightingale made a nuisance[⑨] of herself by insisting that ordinary people deserved to be treated properly, being 'stubborn, opinionated and forthright', according to the director of the Florence Nightingale Museum. But she got things done, which people who ask nicely may not.

In recent years the role of Mary Seacole (1805 – 1881)[⑩] in the Crimean War has become an important topic of discussion. On the one hand she was certainly there at the time, and, at least, dispensed tea and sympathy to people. In 2004 she was voted number one in a poll of black Britons; she appeared on a postage stamp in 2005; a statue was erected in London in 2016; she is part of the national curriculum[⑪]. On the other hand, she certainly did not have the impact that Nightingale did, and some suggest she is remembered more for being black than for any achievements. There was a move, which was defeated, to remove her from the curriculum.

Florence Nightingale will forever be the lady with the lamp, but her whole life was about improving life for ordinary men and women. That goes far beyond the stereotype of a caring, female nurse.

Questions

A Choose the best answer to the questions.

1. What is not true about Florence Nightingale?
  a   She was well-educated.
  b   She did what she wanted to do.
  c   She cared about ordinary soldiers.
  d   She respected rich women.

2. What is true about Florence Nightingale?
  a   She died young.
  b   She had serious health problems.
  c   In later life, illness prevented her from working.
  d   She is buried in Westminster Abbey.

3. How did she care for soldiers in the Crimean War?
  a   physically   b   emotionally
  c   physically and emotionally   d   financially

4. Apart from soldiers' welfare, what did Nightingale campaign for?
  a   tax reform   b   religious freedom
  c   sex workers' welfare   d   education

5. How has Mary Seacole been remembered?
  a   She was an early black Briton.
  b   She's buried in Westminster Abbey.
  c   She was an expert nurse.
  d   She had more influence than Nightingale.

B Write the answers to these questions.

1. Why did Nightingale's mother oppose her ambitions?

2. What made Nightingale famous?

3. How did the ruling class regard ordinary people in Nightingale's day?

4. Why did Nightingale dislike religious hospitals?

5. What caused the Great Stink?

C Decide if the following statements are true or false.

1. Nightingale's most important work was during the Crimean War.

2. She called herself the Lady with the Lamp.

3. She opposed British actions in India.

4. Nightingale was a gentle person.

5. Mary Seacole is part of the school curriculum.

The Lady with the Lamp (Florence Nightingale)
Wikimedia Commons. Photo from Wellcome Images

Chapter 8

Elizabeth Garrett Anderson: Doctor

Elizabeth Garrett Anderson. Wellcome Images.

Elizabeth Garrett Anderson (1836 – 1917)

Elizabeth Garrett Anderson[①] was born in London in 1836. Her ambitious father started with little[②], but became prosperous. Elizabeth received a basic education, with no mathematics or science, but became a keen reader. In 1860 she decided to become a doctor and open up the profession[③] to women. After some hesitation her father decided to give her his full moral and financial support[④].

She studied as a surgery nurse at the Middlesex Hospital[⑤]. The administration also allowed her to study in the dissecting room[⑥], but her male fellow students objected, and she had to leave. She then applied to various medical schools, but was rejected. Eventually she obtained a licence to practise medicine[⑦] in 1865, from the Society of Apothecaries[⑧], which had nothing in its rules to ban women.

Unable to get a job in a hospital, being a woman, she opened her own practice[⑨] in London in 1866, helping women and children of all classes. This became the New Hospital for Women and Children in 1872 (renamed the Elizabeth Garrett

①　Elizabeth Garrett Anderson: 章末注を参照。
②　with little:「ほとんど財産を持たずに」
③　the profession:「専門職」ここでは「医者」
④　moral and financial support:「精神的および財政的支援」
⑤　the Middlesex Hospital: 1745 年に設立され医学教育を行っていた。
⑥　dissecting room:「解剖室」
⑦　practise medicine:「医薬に従事する」動詞の場合イギリスでは practise と綴る。
⑧　the Society of Apothecaries:「薬剤師協会」
⑨　practice:「診療所」

Anderson Hospital in 1918). At this time some men argued that education for women caused nervous and mental disorders and reduced their reproductive capacity[1]. Anderson replied that the real problem for women was boredom and inactivity[2].

After a long career in medicine, Anderson retired to Aldeburgh, Suffolk[3] in 1902, where she is buried.

Her Importance

Elizabeth Garrett Anderson was a lone pioneer, doing studies and taking jobs that were unintentionally[4] open to her, because men had not thought that a woman would do what she did. Often the door was closed behind her. Things are very different today.

In the 1960s in Britain less than 10% of doctors were women. Indeed, the gender divide between male doctors and female nurses was so clear that doctor-nurse romances were a staple[5] of romantic fiction. Now more than 60% of medical students are women, and as of 2017[6] there were more women than men registered as doctors. It seems that, for girls who are good at science, medicine is seen as a suitable career, in a way that, say, engineering still is not. Medicine, ultimately, involves dealing with people; a doctor should have 'a good bedside manner'[7], which is expected of women. Also, people from some religious and ethnic groups expect to be examined by a doctor of the same sex, which is no longer a problem.

The career pattern of many women doctors raises some issues, however. Many women are less willing than many men to work long hours, or to undertake specialisms[8] that require antisocial hours[9]. General practitioners (GPs)[10], doctors who see the general public, work at a practice and largely keep office hours; most of them are women. 50% of consultants (senior doctors) in pediatrics[11] are women; only 12% of consultant surgeons are. Women doctors, like many other women, may take career breaks to have children and then return to work part-time. The average full-time GP earns over £100,000 per year, so part-time work can still provide a good income. 38% of women consultants work part-time; the figure for men is 5%. Anderson herself chose to resign from one position in order to have more time for her children (though she never stopped working).

This raises a number of questions. Should we expect women to work in the same way as men have done? Is it 'natural' for women to devote themselves to childcare in a way that men do not, or is it social pressure? Should modern society be more willing to accept part-time working by both men and women? Does the work-life balance need changing for everyone? Regarding hospitals, should we expect A&E① to be staffed mainly by men? The number of female medical students seems to have settled at just over half, so these questions will remain important.

There is a financial issue. Medical students are no different② from any other students for four years: they must pay for themselves or get a loan. But years five and six are taxpayer funded③, and graduation is followed by two foundation years④ and then further training, which can take up to eight years. Doctors can easily be thirty before being fully qualified. If a lot of doctors end up working part-time, then more doctors will be needed, costing the state more money. This financial issue also includes the question of doctors who train in Britain, but then go and work abroad, for example in Australia or Canada, for higher pay and better conditions. There has been talk of tying medical graduates to jobs in Britain or requiring compensation for taxpayer costs.

Anderson was a pioneer woman doctor. She was also from a wealthy background and privately educated. Today the medical profession remains socially unbalanced. There are plenty of Asian doctors (Asian meaning South Asian⑤, in the British usage), but not many of Afro-Caribbean origin. There are also few doctors from working class backgrounds. It is not easy to spend six years studying, followed by years of rather poorly paid training, unless your family can help you out. Anderson paved the way⑥ for women, but there is still room⑦ for progress.

① **A&E:**「救急治療室」Accident and Emergency の略。

② **no different:**「少しも違わない」not より強い否定。

③ **taxpayer funded:**「納税者の負担・納税者によって資金が提供されている」

④ **foundation years:** 基礎課程の年

⑤ **South Asian:** イギリスの使い方ではインドやパキスタンの人々をさす。

⑥ **pave the way:**「道筋をつける」

⑦ **room:**「余地」

********** NOTES **********

Elizabeth Garrett Anderson: 男になりすまして医師となった James Barry (Margaret Ann Bulkley) を除くと、イギリスで最初の女性医師。suffragist (女性参政権論者) として有名な Millicent Garrett Fawcett の姉。

Questions ··

A Choose the best answer to the questions.

1. How did Anderson's father react to her ambitions?
 a He supported her from the beginning.
 b He opposed her.
 c He refused to give her any money.
 d He paid for her training.

2. What did Anderson think the main problem for women was?
 a having nothing to do
 b being unable to have children
 c mental illness
 d lack of money

3. How many doctors were women in 2017?
 a 10%   b 25%
 c just under 50%   d over 50%

4. What can we say about GPs?
 a They are nearly all men.   b They often work at night.
 c They treat all kinds of patients.   d They are badly paid.

5. From what background are there a lot of doctors?
 a Indian   b Jamaican
 c working class   d Chinese

B Write the answers to these questions.

1. Why did medical schools reject Anderson?

2. Why couldn't Anderson get a hospital job?

3. Why couldn't other women follow Anderson?

4. How are female hospital consultants different from male ones?

5. What are two concerns about taxpayer funding of medical training?

C Decide if the following statements are true or false.

1. Anderson was soon followed by other women doctors.

2. At first, her teachers at Middlesex let her cut up bodies.

3. Female and male doctors have different career patterns.

4. Part-time doctors are a political issue.

5. Anderson didn't stop working when she had children.

Elizabeth Garrett Anderson Hospital. Creative Commons. Photo by Oliver Dixon.

Chapter 9

Octavia Hill: Philanthropist

Octavia Hill
Wikimedia Commons. Wellcome Images

Octavia Hill (1838 – 1912)

 Octavia Hill was born in 1838 in Cambridgeshire①, into a prosperous family. In 1840, however, her father went bankrupt and had a mental collapse②. Octavia was educated at home by her mother. She started work in London at the age of 13, and took over a toy workshop the following year. Through her work she became keenly aware of the poverty of many London children, and the dreadful quality of their housing.

 Hill felt that landlords ignored their duty to their tenants. She saw the relationship as a personal one③, almost a form of social work④. With financial backing she became a landlord herself, and by 1874 she had 15 housing schemes⑤ with over 3,000 tenants. She looked for a return on investment of 5% for her backers, with any surplus reinvested in the housing stock⑥. She opposed government involvement in housing as 'municipal socialism⑦'.

 She also campaigned for more access to open spaces, including in town. She pointed out that Epping Forest⑧, east of London, was indeed a lovely place, but a working person

① **Cambridgeshire:** イングランド東部の州。
② **mental collapse:**「精神的にひどく落ち込んだ状態」
③ **personal one:**「(ビジネスではない)個人的な関係」
④ **a form of social work:**「一種の社会福祉事業」
⑤ **housing schemes:**「(計画的に建てられた)住宅地域」
⑥ **housing stock:**「住宅・住宅建設」
⑦ **municipal socialism:**「都市自治体による社会主義」
⑧ **Epping Forest:** ロンドン東部にある森。もとは王室の猟場であった。

would need to take a day off work, and lose pay, to get there and enjoy it. She was the first person to use the expression 'Green Belt①'.

Hill died in London at the age of 73, and is buried in a rural churchyard in Kent.

Her Importance

Octavia Hill's work centred on improving living conditions for the urban working class. This included the provision of housing and access to open spaces. Both remain important topics today. The Industrial Revolution② led to a great increase in population and a great movement from the countryside to the cities. Conditions in the cities were often terrible, with bad housing, no sanitation③, disease, alcoholism and widespread prostitution. Various people tried to improve these conditions. One was the American banker George Peabody④, who set up the Peabody Trust⑤ in 1862. It still owns and manages 27,000 properties in London. Another one was Joseph Rowntree⑥, of the famous Quaker⑦ chocolate making Rowntree family from York– Rowntree is famous for the Kit Kat. The Joseph Rowntree Foundation (1904) manages 2,000 homes in and around York. So Hill was by no means alone in her efforts. There was, in general, a concern with tenants' lives; after all, a tenant who drinks away his pay⑧ cannot pay rent for himself and his family. Self-reliance⑨ was a key idea.

Individual efforts proved insufficient, however, and the government took over, providing housing throughout the country, including in rural areas. This is known as council housing⑩. Labour⑪ governments have tended to view the provision of decent housing to ordinary people as an end in itself, while Conservative⑫ ones have seen it as a stepping stone to home ownership. Since 1979 much council housing has been sold off, usually to the tenants and often at a discounted price. Council house building has virtually stopped. In London, now, the largest fifteen housing associations⑬ provide housing for one tenth of all Londoners and account for one quarter of all new homes.

① **Green Belt:**「緑地帯」都市周辺に保存されるべき緑地帯。この語は 1875 年 Octavia Hill によって最初に使われた。

② **the Industrial Revolution:**「産業革命」
③ **sanitation:**「衛生設備・下水設備」
④ **George Peabody:**(1795～1869) アメリカの銀行家、社会事業に貢献した。
⑤ **Peabody Trust:** 都市部の住宅環境の改善などに尽力した基金。
⑥ **Joseph Rowntree:** (1836～1925) 慈善事業家。
⑦ **Quaker:**「クエーカー教徒」非暴力・禁酒などを主義とするキリスト教の一派フレンド会 (the Society of Friends) の俗称。創設者 George Fox (1624～91) のことば "to quake at the word of the Lord" によるとの説がある。
⑧ **drinks away his pay:**「給料で酒を飲んでしまう」
⑨ **self-reliance:**「独立独行・他人に頼らないこと」
⑩ **council housing:**「公営住宅」
⑪ **Labour:**「労働党」
⑫ **Conservative:**「保守党」
⑬ **housing association(s):**「住宅建築・購入組合」

It was another of Hill's concerns that Londoners should have access to open spaces, 'to pure earth, clean air and blue sky', as she put it. London has the royal parks, such as Hyde Park[1], in the city centre, but, also, thanks to her, Hampstead Heath[2], a large hillside space in north London, has not been built on. Epping Forest is now easily reached by tube[3]. London has a lot of green space, and it may be noted that in Britain the grass remains green in winter, so these spaces are always green. Since 1947 cities around the country have Green Belt around them, areas of land that may not be built on. This is true of large cities like London, Birmingham and Manchester, but also some smaller ones like Oxford, Cambridge and York. There is always pressure to relax the restrictions on building, but so far[4] it has been resisted.

Hill wanted to 'bring beauty home to the poor'[5]. In 1895 Hill and two others founded The National Trust[6] to preserve historic places and spaces. Today The National Trust has well over 4 million members in England, Wales and Northern Ireland, and 70,000 volunteers. It owns 200 properties, from big houses to old industrial mills, as well as the childhood homes of Paul McCartney and John Lennon. It also owns 2,500 km^2 of land.

One problem is that The National Trust is seen as a white middle class organization, run by the white middle class for the white middle class. Similar concerns are raised about theatre, and about the BBC, particularly its spoken word radio station, Radio 4. There is some truth in this, but it is also true that there are those who regard all culture as middle class. Hill thought that working class people could appreciate art, books and music, as well as open spaces and dignified housing[7]. The National Trust costs money, but not so very much, and Hampstead Heath is open to anyone who can afford the tube fare. Not a bad legacy.

Questions

A Choose the best answer to the questions.

1. How did Hill become aware of the low quality of housing?
   a Her father told her.
   b She lived in bad housing herself.
   c She found out through her work.
   d She read about it.

2. Who funded Hill's housing schemes?
   a investors
   b herself
   c the government
   d the tenants

3. What was not generally true in the cities?
   a There was a lot of drunkenness.
   b Houses had no toilets.
   c There was no work.
   d There was a lot of sickness.

4. How much housing do London housing associations provide?
   a very little
   b 10% of all housing
   c 25% of all housing
   d 75% of all housing

5. Where is The National Trust not active?
   a England
   b Wales
   c Scotland
   d Northern Ireland

B Write the answers to these questions.

1. According to Hill, what was the disadvantage of Epping Forest?

2. Why was it important to prevent alcoholism among tenants?

3. What is council housing?

4. What is important about the Green Belt?

5. What is an image problem for The National Trust?

C Decide if the following statements are true or false.

1. Hill's backers hoped to make a profit.

2. Hill was a Socialist.

3. Hill's work focussed on city conditions.

4. Hyde Park belongs to the government.

5. Hill respected working class people.

Red Cross Cottages, Southwark, London, built by Octavia Hill, 1884-1887.
Creative Commons. Photo by Stephen Richards.

Chapter 10

Gertrude Bell: Adventurer

Gertrude Bell
Wikimedia Commons. Photographer unknown (before 1923).

Gertrude Bell (1868 – 1926)

  Gertrude Bell was born in 1868 in County Durham①, into a wealthy, upper-class family. She received a good education, and gained a degree in history from Oxford University. Fami-
5 ly contacts gave her an early interest in international affairs.

  Bell was a great traveller. She travelled across Arabia six times in twelve years, describing the cities and deserts in widely read writings. She explored ancient sites in Mesopota-mia, and became fluent in many languages, including Arabic
10 and Persian②. She was also a keen mountaineer, once climb-ing Mont Blanc.

  Her expertise③ meant that she was assigned to the British army in the Middle East during World War I. As a Briton she had access to Arab tribal④ leaders, and as a woman she had
15 access to their wives, giving her wider understanding than men. After the collapse of the Ottoman Empire⑤ in 1919, Bell was one of the people responsible for creating new countries in the Middle East, including Iraq. She became an adviser to the new king of Iraq, Faisal⑥.

① **County Durham:**「イングランド北東部の州」

② **Persian:**「ペルシャ語」現代のイラン語。
③ **expertise:**「専門的な知識や経験」
④ **tribal:**「部族の」
⑤ **Ottoman Empire:**「オスマン帝国・オスマントルコ帝国」13世紀にOsman Iによって創設された帝国。最盛期にはアジア、アフリカ、ヨーロッパにまたがる大帝国となった。
⑥ **Faisal:**「(イラク王)ファイサル1世」Faisal Iは、第一次世界大戦時にオスマン帝国に対する反乱が起きた際のアラブの指導者であった。

Bell overworked herself, suffered from malaria, and was a heavy smoker. She died in Baghdad in 1926, and is buried there. Her funeral was a major event, attended by King Faisal, among many others①.

Her Importance

In the days of the British empire there were many people like Gertrude Bell②. There was much to admire about them: they were intrepid③ and fearless, physically daring④, multilingual, with great knowledge of other cultures, and often great admiration for those cultures. This was particularly true of Arab culture, with the classic example being T. E. Lawrence⑤, generally known as Lawrence of Arabia, whom Bell met. Such people also had feelings of class and racial superiority, which made them feel entitled to be in control of others⑥.

There was a nineteenth and early twentieth century rivalry⑦ between Britain and Russia for control of Central Asia, a rivalry that stretched from the Middle East through Iran and Afghanistan to western China (Xinjiang⑧, or Chinese Turkestan⑨). This was known as the Great Game⑩. It was a game to some British adventurers, a dangerous one, but hardly a game to the local people. So the really unusual thing about Bell is that she was a woman, one whose actions still affect the Middle East today.

Empires, whether Roman, Persian, Songhai⑪ or Inca, generally managed to rule fairly well over multiethnic⑫, multilingual, multireligious territories. This has proved much more difficult for nations. When the Ottoman empire collapsed after World War I, the British (and French) took control of much of the Middle East and tried to create nations by dividing it up.

When Iraq was created it contained Sunni and Shia Muslims⑬, part of the Kurdish region⑭, as well as other religious groups, including Christians, Jews and Yazidis⑮. The current ethnic and religious warfare can be seen as going back to the decisions Bell and others took. There is nothing to unite all of the people, and much to divide them. Multiethnic societies like the USA and Britain seem divided by ethnicity⑯ and religion, even by language, but share values and ideas, symbolized by the flag in America and the Queen in Britain. Iraq has no such values and ideas. And Iraq is not unique in its problems: many postcolonial[①] societies, from Nigeria to Korea, have had great difficulty in creating a united nation.

   Another side of Bell and others is globalism. In school, British children learn that the English and Scots were latecomers to global exploration, after the Spanish and Portuguese. After that, however, they learn of a long history of adventure, from Francis Drake[②] in the sixteenth century, to Captain (James) Cook[③] in the eighteenth, and on to Dr. (David) Livingstone[④] and Mungo Park[⑤] in Africa in the nineteenth. Even failures were heroic: Captain (Robert) Scott[⑥], Scott of the Antarctic, died in a snowstorm, along with all his companions, on the way back from the South Pole in 1912, but is remembered for a noble death (rather than incompetence[⑦]). Mountain climbing is also part of this adventurous spirit: fun, dangerous and in this case rather pointless. Bell herself once spent 48 hours on a rope in a snowstorm in the Alps. The conquest of Everest in 1953 is a famous British triumph, even if the conquerors were a New Zealander and a Nepalese. Another aspect of such people as Bell is cultural and scientific. The British Museum is full of things taken – perhaps bought, perhaps stolen – from other countries. The botanical gardens at Kew[⑧], near London, contain species from around the world, often obtained with great difficulty. Part of Captain Cook's work was to observe a transit of Venus[⑨] from Tahiti in 1769.

   Bell's travel writings are well known, and there continues to be a rich tradition of such writing. TV travel programmes are popular, too. Many young people take a 'gap year[⑩]' between school and university to travel the world. Many British people are ready to live abroad for considerable periods. Bell is one example of a continuing tradition: the global Briton.

---

① **postcolonial:**「（ヨーロッパの）植民地支配以後の」
② **Francis Drake:** (1540?～96) エリザベス朝のイングランドの航海者、海賊、海軍提督。イギリス人として初めて世界一周を達成し、アルマダの海戦ではスペインの無敵艦隊を打ち破った。
③ **Captain (James) Cook:** (1728～79) イギリス人探検家ジェームズ・クック（通称キャプテン・クック）はイングランド中部の出身。水兵として海軍に参加、測量士として頭角を現し、エンデバー号を指揮して太平洋航海を3回行い、南アメリカ最南端やハワイ諸島に到達、ハワイで先住民とのトラブルの末に死亡した。
④ **David Livingstone:** (1813～73) スコットランドの探検家、宣教師、医師。ヨーロッパ人で初めて、アフリカ大陸を横断し、アフリカでの奴隷解放へ向けて尽力した。
⑤ **Mungo Park:** (1771～1806) スコットランド人の探検家。アフリカのニジェール川中央部を探検した。
⑥ **Captain (Robert) Scott:** (1868～1912) イギリス海軍の軍人。南極探検家「南極のスコット」として名をはせ、1912年に南極点到達を果たしたが、その帰途で遭難し死亡した。
⑦ **incompetence:**「無能・不適格」
⑧ **The botanical gardens at Kew:**「キュー植物園」ロンドン南西部のキューにある王立植物園。宮殿併設の庭園として始まり、今ではユネスコ世界遺産に登録されている。18世紀後半から「プラント・ハンター」と呼ばれる人々が世界中から植物の種子や苗を持ち帰った。
⑨ **a transit of Venus:**「金星の太陽面通過」
⑩ **gap year:**「ギャップイヤー」高校卒業後、大学入学資格を保持したまま1年間遊学したり社会で働いたりすることができる制度。

Questions

A Choose the best answer to the questions.

1. **What was not one of Bell's interests?**
   - a languages
   - b archaeology
   - c cooking
   - d writing

2. **What was not one of Bell's health problems?**
   - a overwork
   - b tropical disease
   - c smoking
   - d alcoholism

3. **How was Bell unusual among British adventurers?**
   - a She spoke many languages.
   - b She was a woman.
   - c She admired the Arabs.
   - d She felt socially confident.

4. **What is not a religious group in Iraq?**
   - a the Kurds
   - b the Yazidis
   - c Sunni people
   - d Shia people

5. **Who died of cold?**
   - a Drake
   - b Cook
   - c Livingstone
   - d Scott

B Write the answers to these questions.

1. What three attributes helped Bell with Arab politics?

2. What is less attractive about people like Bell?

3. Who took part in the Great Game?

4. What unites the British?

5. What do many young British people do in their gap year?

C Decide if the following statements are true or false.

1. King Faisal respected Bell.

2. British men could talk to Arab tribal leaders' wives.

3. Bell helped create modern Middle Eastern countries about 100 years ago.

4. A British man was the first person on top of Mount Everest.

5. Kew gardens contain plants from all over the world.

Gertrude Bell, Winston Churchill (left), and T. E. Lawrence (Lawrence of Arabia), Egypt. Citizendium. 1921 photo. Out of copyright.

Chapter 11

Marie Stopes: Sexologist

Marie Stopes
Photo before 1923. Out of copyright.

Marie Stopes (1880 – 1958)

Marie Stopes was born in Edinburgh in 1880, into an intellectual family. She grew up in London, where she met many famous scholars, and gained a degree in botany and geology from University College, London. In her early career she was a paleobotanist①, work which included eighteen months in Japan (1907 – 1908), exploring coal mines in Hokkaido for fossilized plants.

Stopes married in 1911, but the marriage soon failed. More to the point②, it seems to have taken her some time to realize that the marriage had never been consummated③. In 1918, to fight this kind of ignorance, she published *Married Love*, which discussed women's sexual pleasure and advocated birth control, previously taboo topics. It was a huge success, going through six printings④ in two weeks. Many readers, by no means⑤ all women, wrote to her for advice, which she tried to give. In her next book she gave clear advice on contraceptive methods⑥, which aroused strong opposition from many, mainly male, Christians. She opened a Mothers' Clinic in London

① paleobotanist:「化石植物学者」

② More to the point:「もっと適切に言えば・もっとはっきり言えば」
③ consummated: consummate =「（性的な関係を結び結婚を）完全なものとする」
④ going through six printings:「6刷までいった」
⑤ by no means:「決して〜ではない」
⑥ contraceptive methods:「避妊法」

in 1921.

Stopes opposed abortion, which she regarded as murder. She also supported the forced sterilization[1] of those 'unfit for parenthood', meaning lower class women. She died in 1958, leaving her clinic to the Eugenics Society[2].

Her Importance

The success of Marie Stopes' book *Married Love* shows how necessary it was, and how many people lived in ignorance of basic facts about sex, birth control and childbirth. Stopes knew from her own experience how important it was for women, in particular, to have control of their fertility[3].

Today sex and relationship education (SRE) is compulsory[4] in British secondary schools (age 11 and up), where it is part of the science curriculum. The government says SRE teaches 'reproduction[5], sexuality and sexual health'. It is an area of controversy. Some, mostly religious, people feel it encourages early sexual activity, sex outside marriage and homosexuality. Others feel it should start much earlier (as in The Netherlands), and should include more guidance on relationships and on safety, particularly with regard to the Internet.

Teenage pregnancy[6] rates in Britain have halved since 2007, perhaps the result of education, but perhaps also the result of changes in social activity. Certainly young people are drinking less and communicating far more by social media. On the other hand the number of live births[7] to girls aged 15 to 17, while low, is six times as high in the UK as in Denmark. Clearly more knowledge and, it seems, less embarrassment are needed.

British women have more control of their own fertility than ever before. Numerous contraceptive methods are available free from the National Health Service[8]. Abortion is also generally available without cost, and abortion is not the emotive issue it is in the USA, except in religious Northern Ireland[9], where it remains illegal. It is a common procedure, with around 190,000 carried out in 2015, 70% of them to women in a stable relationship[10] (contrary to the public image of foolish

---

[1] **sterilization:**「避妊手術」
[2] **the Eugenics Society:** 1907年 the Eugenics Education Societyとして設立、1926年に the Eugenics Societyとなった。当初は優生学の研究などを行ったが、その後優生学がナチスに利用され、また人種差別にもつながることから批判された。現在は the Galton Society と名を変え、その目的を「遺伝についての理解を推し進め、生殖技術の進歩に伴う倫理的問題を広く議論する」と規定している。
[3] **fertility:**「出産能力」
[4] **compulsory:**「必修の」
[5] **reproduction:**「生殖」
[6] **pregnancy:**「妊娠」
[7] **live birth(s):**「生産児」
[8] **the National Health Service:**「(イギリスの)国民保険サーヴィス」第二次大戦後1948年から実施され、基本的に医療費は無料であったが、1957年からは若干の費用負担がある。
[9] **Northern Ireland:** 北アイルランドにはカトリック教徒の住民が多く、カトリックは妊娠中絶を認めていない。
[10] **stable relationship:** 結婚や同棲などの安定した男女関係。

teenagers). Persuading men to take responsibility, and promoting forms of contraception aimed at men – a male pill, for example – have been less successful.

Stopes was opposed to abortion (and to divorce), which is one reason why she is not the feminist icon she might be. Another less pleasant side of her thinking can be summed up as eugenics. She was aware of people having too many children they could ill afford to keep, and her response was to want to discourage the poor ('the worst' as she called them) from breeding. She was in favour of compulsory sterilization[①] of 'unfit' women. She was not alone in this: four north European countries adopted eugenics, and such famous people as the economist Keynes[②] and the writer Shaw[③] advocated it. There was a fear of 'racial darkness[④]', with Catholics (Irish) and Jews (from Eastern Europe), as well as lower class people, coming to outnumber the socially and racially superior.

Eugenics has been discredited[⑤] (not least[⑥] by Nazi policies[⑦]), but these fears persist. The image of the feckless[⑧] teenage girl with numerous children by numerous fathers, living high on benefits[⑨], is a powerful one which some newspapers like to exploit. Immigrants are thought to have far more children than natives, and it is true that in 2015 27.5% of live births in the UK were to women born abroad. The three most common nationalities were Polish (Catholic), Pakistani (Muslim) and Indian (various). Catholicism and Islam both oppose birth control. In Northern Ireland some Protestants think that Catholics will outbreed[⑩] them and then vote to join the Republic of Ireland[⑪]. There is a fear of being 'swamped[⑫]'.

According to government statistics, class actually seems to have no bearing[⑬] on family size, while black and Asian, particularly Muslim, families are larger than white ones. It seems likely that future generations will become native and follow native custom.

Stopes had a huge impact in the struggle for sexual knowledge and control, especially for women, but that fine legacy is tainted by some unpleasant attitudes[⑭] which, unfortunately, still persist.

---

① **compulsory sterilization:**「強制的な不妊手術」
② **Keynes:** John Maynard Keynes（1883〜1946）。イギリスの経済学者。彼の著書『雇用・利子および貨幣の一般理論』(1936) は経済学に「ケインズ革命」と言われるほど大きな影響を与えた。
③ **Shaw:** George Bernard Shaw（1856〜1950）。アイルランド生まれのイギリスの劇作家。1925 年にはノーベル文学賞を受賞。
④ **racial darkness:** Marie Stopes のことばの中に出てくる表現。労働者階級やカトリックの人々が子だくさんであることを悲観して述べた表現。
⑤ **discredited:**「信用を傷つけられる」
⑥ **not least:**「とりわけ」
⑦ **Nazi policies:** 章末注を参照
⑧ **feckless:**「無責任な・軽率な」
⑨ **on benefits:**「給付金を受けて」
⑩ **outbreed:**「〜より子孫を増やす」
⑪ **the Republic of Ireland:**「アイルランド共和国」1949 年にイギリスから独立。
⑫ **swamped:**「圧倒される」
⑬ **bearing:**「関係・関連」
⑭ **unpleasant attitudes:** 現在も残る Stopes が持っていたような人種的階級的偏見。

********** NOTES **********

Nazi policies:「ナチスの政策」ナチスはドイツ民族の優秀性を宣伝し、それを維持するという名目でユダヤ人の虐殺を行った。また、長身、金髪、碧眼の青年どうしを結婚させてドイツ民族の改良まで試みようとした。

Questions ··

A Choose the best answer to the questions.

1. What was the young Stopes most interested in?
   - a coal
   - b living plants
   - c Japan
   - d plant fossils

2. What was the purpose of *Married Love*?
   - a to give women knowledge about sex
   - b to encourage women to leave their husbands
   - c to persuade women to have more children
   - d to encourage single women to have sex

3. What information do some people think SRE should also include?
   - a information about birth control
   - b reasons why homosexuality is normal
   - c ways to avoid disease
   - d ways to stay safe online

4. Where in the UK is abortion not permitted?
   - a England
   - b Wales
   - c Scotland
   - d Northern Ireland

5. Why is Stopes not a hero to many feminists?
   - a She opposed birth control.
   - b She opposed abortion.
   - c She opposed eugenics.
   - d She opposed Keynes and Shaw.

B Write the answers to these questions.

1. What first pushed Stopes to write *Married Love*?

2. Why did many Christians oppose Stopes?

3. Why do some people dislike SRE in schools?

4. Why was Stopes in favour of eugenics?

5. Why might Catholics and Muslims have a lot of children?

C Decide if the following statements are true or false.

1. Stopes thought abortion was murder.

2. Primary school children study SRE.

3. Teenage pregnancy rates have fallen greatly.

4. Abortion is generally accepted in mainland Britain.

5. Family size varies according to social class.

Blue Plaque on Stopes' childhood home.
Wikimedia Commons. Photo by Edwardx.

Chapter 12

Lily Parr: Footballer

Lily Parr (1905 – 1978)

Lily Parr was born in St Helens, Lancashire[①] in 1905, into a working class family. She was a strong and fearless child, and had no interest in cooking and sewing, preferring to play football and rugby with her elder brothers.

She started playing football professionally at the age of 14 in 1919, just after the First World War. She was given a job in a factory in Preston, Lancashire, and played football for the factory team, Dick, Kerr Ladies[②], at the weekends. In her first season she scored 43 goals, despite being a winger[③]. While many men were away at war, women's football became popular, and remained so for a while. In 1920 Parr played in a game at Goodison Park[④], Liverpool (Everton's ground) in front of 53,000 people, with another 14,000 unable to get in.

In the same year she played several times for England against France. She also played against male teams, something that does not happen now. In 1921 the Football Association[⑤] banned women from playing on member grounds, and women's football faded. Parr, however, while working as a nurse,

---

[①] **Lancashire:** イングランド北西部の州。工業地帯として知られる。

[②] **Dick, Kerr Ladies:** 章末注を参照。

[③] **winger:**「ウイングの選手」forward（前衛）の両端の守備位置にいる選手。したがって攻撃の前面にたつ forward ほどはゴールを決めることはない。

[④] **Goodison Park:** 章末注を参照。

[⑤] **the Football Association:** 章末注を参照。

continued playing until 1951.

Openly lesbian, Parr has become an LGBT[①] hero. In 2002 she was the only woman among the inaugural inductees[②] into the English Football Hall of Fame[③]. She is buried in St Helens.

Her Importance

Lily Parr is not a household name[④], but her career illustrates a number of points. The first one, not directly connected to sport, involves the role of women during the First World War. A huge number of men were sent to fight, and women were brought in to do jobs previously regarded as men's jobs, including dangerous, unhealthy work in munitions factories[⑤]. After the war such jobs were given back to men, just as football once more became a male sport.

Few sportswomen ever become famous, particularly in team sports. Perhaps the only women's sports that the general public[⑥] are interested in are athletics[⑦] and tennis. If a women's team does well, there may be interest for a while: there was some excitement when the British women's hockey team won the gold medal at the 2016 Rio Olympics, for example.

This is not for want of[⑧] trying. Sport is a central part of the British school curriculum, in a way that it is not in other European countries. Girls, like boys, have to do PE[⑨] and take part in team sports. On the other hand, teenage girls can be rather self-conscious[⑩] about their bodies, and may get teased by boys, leading them to avoid sport whenever possible. Physical exertion[⑪] can still seem unladylike; as the old saying goes, "Horses sweat, men perspire, but women simply glow[⑫]". More generally, schools are being forced by financial pressure to sell off their playing fields, so the future of school team sports is in doubt.

For adult men, there are plenty of opportunities for team sports. A lot of men play football, often in so-called pub leagues, as the team is often organized by a local pub; or they play cricket, perhaps in the city, but idealized as the village team. There are few company teams. Individual sports, such as tennis, golf, swimming and running, are popular with both

---

[①] **LGBT:** レズビアン(lesbian)、ゲイ(gay)、バイセクシャル(bisexual)、トランスジェンダー(transgender)の英語の頭文字から作られたセクシャルマイノリティの総称。

[②] **inaugural inductees:**「当初から殿堂に入った人たち」

[③] **the English Football Hall of Fame:** 章末注を参照。

[④] **household name:**「おなじみの名前」

[⑤] **munitions factory:**「軍需工場」

[⑥] **general public:**「一般大衆」

[⑦] **athletics:**「陸上競技」

[⑧] **for want of:**「~が不足しているから」

[⑨] **PE:**「(Physical Education)体育の授業」

[⑩] **self-conscious:**「自意識の強い・~を気にする」

[⑪] **exertion:**「激しい活動」

[⑫] **Horses sweat, men perspire, but women simply glow:** 章末注を参照。

sexes. In the countryside horse riding is popular, though rather expensive. Cycling has become more popular recently, both as a sport and as a method of commuting①, though people are concerned about the dangers. Walking is the most popular sport, if it is a sport. The country has a large network of public footpaths② and public rights of way③ across farms and mountainsides. The walking group The Ramblers④ has well over 100,000 members. Nonetheless, British people are among the fattest in the world, and it is clear that a lot of people do not get enough exercise.

A major reason for the success of women's football one hundred years ago was gambling. Sport has always involved gambling, often over animals, as we still see with horse-racing, but also people. People gambled on football, and women's football enabled that to continue. Today gambling on sport is widespread, with betting shops in every town, and a remarkable number of racecourses. It is a global phenomenon, and there is considerable corruption, with frequent accusations⑤ of match-fixing⑥ (it has happened in professional tennis). Cricket poses a particular difficulty, being a slow game with many different elements. To fix the result⑦ of a cricket game can easily lead to suspicion, but individual players can be paid to perform badly, and that is hard to spot.

Lily Parr and her team-mates played in front of crowds numbering over 50,000. That remains the case for Premier League football. TV companies pay huge sums of money to secure the broadcasting rights, and top players can be paid tens of thousands of⑧ pounds per week. Organized sport⑨ has been a central part of British culture for at least 250 years, and that is not about to change.

---

① **commuting:**「通勤・通学」
② **public footpath:** イギリスの農村部を中心に、網の目のように走っている公共の遊歩道。牧場などの私有地の中を人々が昔から歩いて利用していた道に現在でも通行権を認めている。
③ **public rights of way:**「公共権利通路」ある土地が私有地であっても、公衆の通路として長く使われてきて、現在も使われ続けているのであれば、誰もが自由にそこを通路として利用する権利があるという考えに基づく。public footpath よりも広い概念で public footpath もその中に含まれる。
④ **The Ramblers:** ウォーキングを促進しているイギリスのチャリティー団体。
⑤ **accusation:**「告発」
⑥ **match-fixing:**「八百長」
⑦ **fix the result:**「八百長をする」
⑧ **tens of thousands of:**「何万という」

⑨ **organized sport:**「(観客などを動員するために) 組織されたスポーツ」

✽✽✽✽✽✽✽✽✽✽ NOTES ✽✽✽✽✽✽✽✽✽✽

Dick, Kerr Ladies: 1917 年創設の女子フットボールチーム。軍需工場 Dick, Kerr & Co. Ltd の女子従業員たちによって作られたクラブチーム。試合によって得られた収益を第一次大戦の負傷兵のために寄付した。football は日本でいう soccer のこと。
Goodison Park: イングランド北西部の町リヴァプールにあるサッカー・スタジアム。現在は Everton FC の本拠地となっている。
the Football Association:「サッカー協会」1863 年に設立され、サッカーのルールを決めるなど協会メンバーを統括した。現在は Premier League の運営等も行っている。
the English Football Hall of Fame:「イングランドサッカー殿堂」イングランドのサッカー界で活躍が認められた選手と指導者が表彰される。イングランドで 5 年以上プレイした選手や、監督を務めた指導者で、年齢などの条件も設けられている。
Horses sweat, men perspire, but women simply glow: ことわざ「馬は汗をかき、男性は発汗し、女性は火照る」の意。sweat、perspire、glow という 3 種類の動詞を使って「汗のかきかた」を表現している。馬、男性、女性と後になるほどより上品な言い方となっている。

Questions

A Choose the best answer to the questions.

1. **In what position did Parr play?**
   a goalkeeper   b defence
   c midfield   d attack

2. **When did Parr play for England?**
   a 1919   b 1920
   c 1921   d 1951

3. **What women's sport is popular to watch?**
   a tennis   b hockey
   c football   d golf

4. **What sport do we imagine to be played by the village team?**
   a cricket   b football
   c rugby   d hockey

5. **What sport is most popular to gamble on?**
   a horse racing   b golf
   c cycling   d rugby

B Write the answers to these questions.

1. Why did women stop playing football in big stadiums?

2. What dangerous work did many women do during the First World War?

3. How is the British school curriculum different from that of many other European countries?

4. What makes walking in the countryside easy in Britain?

5. Which British sport is the richest?

C Decide if the following statements are true or false.

1. Parr played against men.

2. Lily Parr hid her sexuality.

3. In the First World War women made weapons.

4. The British are overweight.

5. Sports gambling causes problems.

Lily Parr. Pictures of footballers on cards were given away with cigarettes, for fans to collect.

Chapter 13

Elizabeth David: Food Writer

Elizabeth David (1913 − 1992) as a girl (Elizabeth Gwynne) in 1923.
Portrait by Ambrose McEvoy (1878 − 1927).

Elizabeth David (1913 – 1992)

Elizabeth David was born in Sussex① in 1913, into a wealthy, upper class family. She was educated at boarding school② before studying at the Sorbonne③ in Paris. She lodged with a French family who loved food, starting a lifelong interest.

David rebelled against family expectations and became an actress. In 1939 she ran off④ with a married man, travelling through France, Italy and Greece, before ending up in wartime Cairo. Throughout this trip she was learning more about good food. She eventually returned from the sunny Mediterranean to a drab, depressed England, a country with terrible food, in 1946. In 1950 she published *A Book Of Mediterranean Food*, which was an immediate success. It was not just an illustrated collection of recipes, but also a history. It also called for⑤ aubergines⑥, basil, figs⑦, garlic, olive oil and saffron, so for most people in Britain the recipes were impossible but inspiring⑧.

From then until 1984 she continued writing and publishing books and articles on food, and was regarded as the authority

① **Sussex:** 1974 年までイングランド南部にあった州。現在は West Sussex と East Sussex の二つの州に分かれている。
② **boarding school:** 寄宿制の学校。
③ **the Sorbonne:** 旧パリ大学文学部の通称。現在ではパリ第 4 大学の通称となっている。
④ **run off:**「駆け落ちする」
⑤ **call for:**「求める・必要とする」
⑥ **aubergine(s):**「ナス」イギリス英語。米語では **eggplant**
⑦ **fig(s):**「イチジク」
⑧ **inspiring:**「(何かを)促すような・鼓舞するような」

on the Mediterranean. She died in 1992 and is buried where she grew up, in Sussex. In 2012, the sixtieth year of the reign of Queen Elizabeth II, David was voted one of the 60 most influential Britons.

Her Importance

Historically, Britain had plenty of good food, particularly meat, but the Industrial Revolution led to many people eating very bad food. In the 1930s it was suggested that Indian peasants were better fed than the British working class. During and after the Second World War food was rationed①. After the war British food tended to consist of overcooked meat, boiled potatoes and watery vegetables. Wine was very unusual. There was some limited Indian influence, such as in mulligatawny② soup and kedgeree③, but foreign food was generally unknown or regarded with suspicion. The food was dull, and people seemed to eat to live, rather than regarding food as a pleasure.

Rich people had used olive oil for some time, but it was not widely available, and David famously suggested getting olive oil from pharmacies④, where it was sold in small bottles as a remedy⑤ for earache⑥. *A Book Of Mediterranean Food* must have seemed impossibly exotic to many people. David was not alone, though: 1951 saw⑦ the first publication of *The Good Food Guide*, which advocated eating British food but cooking it properly.

In the 70 years since then, British food has been transformed. This is partly because of money and modern transportation: people can afford exotic food, which can easily be brought from all over the world. It is partly from the experience of foreign food gained from foreign holidays⑧ and from immigrants opening restaurants. But mostly it is from a change in attitude. Garlic is no longer something Frenchmen stink of⑨; it is not unmanly to drink wine; Chinese noodles are not foreign muck⑩, fit only to be eaten outside. Supermarkets carry a tremendous range of foods, from France, Italy, Lebanon, Japan, Mexico and elsewhere. There are guidebooks to supermarket wines, such is the variety.

① **rationed:**「配給される・割り当てられる」
② **mulligatawny:** インドのカレースープ。マリガトニースープ。
③ **kedgeree:** 香辛料などを使ったインド料理。ケジャリー。
④ **pharmacies:** pharmacy=「薬局」
⑤ **remedy:**「治療薬」
⑥ **earache:**「耳の痛み」
⑦ **saw:** 時代等を主語にして see =「(その時代に)起こる・(その時代が)経験する」
⑧ **foreign holidays:**「外国への休暇旅行・外国での休暇」
⑨ **stink of:**「〜の臭いがする・〜臭い」
⑩ **muck:**「不潔なもの」

David said cooking should not be a drudgery①, but an exciting and creative act. The large number of celebrity chefs suggests that many people agree. Bookshops have large cookery sections; newspapers have restaurant critics; there is renewed interest in local specialities②. Most famous is the cosy③ TV show *The Great British Bake Off*, in which ordinary people compete, over several weeks, to be the best baker. It was headline news when a woman of Bangladeshi origin won, and when it moved to a different TV channel. The programme has increased interest in cake baking, and mildly risqué④ jokes about soggy bottoms⑤ (cakes or people?) have become well known.

On the other hand, many people continue to eat very badly. They eat a lot of fast foods, processed convenience foods, foods that just need warming in the microwave, and foods containing a lot of fat or sugar. Even basic foods like bread contain sugar these days. Fresh food is expensive and requires preparation, and there are those who see no reason to peel vegetables. For them, cooking remains a drudgery. There are homes without a dining table because people always eat in front of the TV. Following concern over childhood obesity⑥ and the quality of school meals, one TV chef was brought in to improve the meals at a school in London. However, some parents were seen bringing bags of chips⑦ for their children and passing them over the school fence. There is clearly a great division⑧ in eating habits.

In general, though, food writers have had a great effect on British eating habits, with David the famous pioneer. In the past, girls would learn to cook at school, while boys would not. Greater gender equality in education means that now nobody learns to cook at school, and few do at home, either. Most young people learn to cook from cookbooks; fortunately there is no shortage of those.

---

① **drudgery:**「つまらない仕事」

② **local specialities:**「土地の名物料理」

③ **cosy:**「楽しくくつろいだ雰囲気の」

④ **risqué:**「(性的に)きわどい」

⑤ **bottoms:** bottom に「(ケーキの)下側」と「(人間の)臀部」とをかけたもの。

⑥ **obesity:**「肥満」

⑦ **chips:** アメリカでは日本と同様のポテトチップスを指すが、イギリスでは日本でいうフライドポテトを指す。ここでは後者。

⑧ **division:**「(見解などの)相違」

Questions

A Choose the best answer to the questions.

1. Where did David first learn to love food?
   a England
   b France
   c Italy
   d Greece

2. When did Elizabeth II become queen?
   a 1946
   b 1952
   c 1992
   d 2012

3. What was not a general part of British food after the war?
   a overcooked meat
   b potatoes
   c watery vegetables
   d wine

4. What is the main reason for the improvement in British food?
   a People have more money.
   b People travel abroad.
   c People's thinking has changed.
   d People watch TV cooking programmes.

5. What is not mentioned as a food problem?
   a processed food
   b fatty food
   c salty food
   d sweetened food

B Write the answers to these questions.

1. What possibly dangerous thing did the young David do?

2. What was David's favourite sea?

3. What was one effect of the Industrial Revolution?

4. What was olive oil used for just after the Second World War?

5. What do people cook on *The Great British Bake Off?*

C Decide if the following statements are true or false.

1. David did not travel beyond Europe.

2. Food rationing continued after the war.

3. There is Japanese food in British supermarkets.

4. Many people are interested in good food.

5. Many people eat badly.

Chapter 14

Ruth Ellis: Murderer

Ruth Ellis (1926 – 1955)

    Ruth Ellis was born in North Wales, but grew up in Hampshire①. She left school at 14② and worked as a waitress. In 1941, at the height of German bombing③, her family moved to London. Ellis became pregnant and had a son in 1944.

    She took up④ nude modelling work and became a night club hostess, which paid better than office work. Later she moved into prostitution⑤. In 1950 she married, but her husband proved to be jealous, alcoholic and violent, and the marriage ended.

    In 1953 she became a night club manager, where she met David Blakely⑥, who soon moved in with her⑦. Both of them, however, continued to see other people. Blakely became jealous and violent, and Ellis had a miscarriage after he punched her in the stomach.

    On 10th April, 1955, Ellis followed Blakely to a pub in north London, and waited outside until he came out. She had a revolver⑧, and shot at him, but missed. She fired again and he collapsed. She went over to⑨ him and fired three more times.

---

① **Hampshire:** イングランド南岸の州。
② **left school at 14:** leave school は日本語でいう「退学する」場合にも「卒業する」場合にも使われる。
③ **at the height of German bombing:**「ドイツ軍の爆撃の真っ最中に」
④ **took up:**「始めた」take up =「(趣味や仕事などを)始める・取りかかる」
⑤ **prostitution:**「売春」
⑥ **David Blakely:** 章末注を参照。
⑦ **moved in with her:**「彼女の家に転がり込んだ」in は副詞。

⑧ **revolver:**「リボルバー・回転式連発拳銃」
⑨ **went over to:**「〜に近づいた」

The sixth shot ricocheted off[1] the ground and injured a passer-by[2]. Ellis was immediately arrested.

She was found guilty of murder, sentenced to death, and hanged on 13th July, 1955, the last woman to be hanged in Britain.

Her Importance

The Ruth Ellis case was sensational at the time, and, since she was the last woman in Britain to be hanged, has remained prominent. Then, she received considerable sympathy, as a victim of long-running[3] violence, but also as a glamorous[4] woman (other less attractive women murderers at the time received little interest). More recently, some have suggested she was hanged because she was a woman, and that a man would not have been hanged in those circumstances. Some also suggest that women think and feel differently from men, and that a law designed for men should not have applied to her.

It was clearly a premeditated crime[5], and Ellis herself said at her trial[6] that she intended to kill Blakely. The jury took just 25 minutes to convict her, and the death sentence was mandatory – the judge had no option. Yet the death sentence was often not carried out. Between 1926 and 1954 (Ellis' lifetime, basically) in England and Wales 677 men were sentenced to death and 375 were executed, while 60 women were sentenced to death, of whom only 7 were executed. The Home Secretary[7] could have reprieved[8] her, but chose not to, perhaps because Ellis fired a gun in a public place and injured a passing woman (handguns have always been rare in the UK). The decision is still questioned.

The case continues to illustrate a number of issues. One is whether the criminal justice[9] system discriminates against women. Regarding the past, the statistics on executions above[10] strongly suggest otherwise. Current statistics on sentencing also suggest that women are treated more leniently[11] than men.

Another question is the existence of the death penalty. It was last used in the UK in 1964, and was abolished in Britain in 1969 (1973 in Northern Ireland). Murder rates rose after that, until 2002, and then fell sharply. For a long time it remained controversial, and the public supported bringing back capital punishment①. In Parliament, however, politicians were given a free vote on the matter, meaning that they could vote as they chose, rather than doing what their party leader told them to do. The result was always against a restoration②. Today it is not a prominent issue, indeed it seems rather uncivilized, and there is no likelihood③ of its being brought back.

A third question concerns mandatory sentences④. In Ellis' case the judge had no choice. Today murder carries a mandatory life sentence⑤. Life, however, does not usually mean life. Depending on the crime it can mean a minimum of fifteen years, or thirty, or in rare cases actually the criminal's whole life, usually for the protection of the public⑥. Within these limits judges have considerable power to set sentences, and politicians (including the Home Secretary) may not interfere. So the judiciary⑦ is more independent of the legislature⑧ than it was in Ellis' day.

Protection of the public is one reason to put people in prison, or to execute them. Another is control of revenge; personal vengeance⑨ leads to violence and chaos, so the government has a monopoly on punishment. Yet another is illustrated by the Scottish legal system⑩, which does not allow whole life sentences, but calls for 'satisfying the requirements of retribution and deterrence⑪'. In a way, the two things are similar: fear of retribution, or punishment, should prevent people from committing crimes, while the example of the punishment given to others should also make people think twice⑫ about breaking the law. Ellis planned the murder, made no attempt to escape, admitted intending to kill, and remained calm in the face of death; so it seems that nothing would have deterred her.

---

① **capital punishment:**「死刑・極刑」death penalty、death sentence などと同義。
② **a restoration:**「(もとの状態への)復活」
③ **likelihood:**「見込み・可能性」
④ **mandatory sentence(s):**「選択の余地のない判決・判事などの裁量が許されない判決」
⑤ **a mandatory life sentence:**「裁量が許されずに確定される終身刑」
⑥ **for the protection of the public:**「一般の人びとの身の安全のために」
⑦ **judiciary:**「司法」
⑧ **legislature:**「立法府」
⑨ **vengeance:**「復讐・敵討ち」
⑩ **the Scottish legal system:** Scotland は England とは異なる法体系を持っている。
⑪ **satisfying the requirements of retribution and deterrence:**「悪行などに対する相応の報復と(犯罪の)抑止の両方の役割を満たす」
⑫ **think twice:**「よく考える・再考する」

********** NOTES **********

David Blakely: Ruth Ellis による殺人の被害者。Ruth が働くナイトクラブで出会った二人はすぐに交際を始めるが、その時 David は妻帯者であった。ハンサムで裕福なレーシングドライバーである David は、他の女性からも人気があり、そのことで争いが絶えず、次第に Ruth はアルコールに依存するようになる。

Questions ....

A Choose the best answer to the questions.

1. What is true about the murder Ellis committed?
   a She planned it.
   b She shot Blakely six times.
   c She escaped from the scene.
   d She shot Blakely outside his home.

2. How many violent partners did Ellis have?
   a one   b two
   c three   d four

3. Why did Ellis receive the death sentence?
   a The public demanded it.   b The jury imposed it.
   c The judge chose it.   d The law required it.

4. When was the death penalty last used?
   a 1956   b 1964
   c 1969   d 1973

5. Who has generally supported the death penalty?
   a the general public   b politicians
   c lawyers   d nobody

B Write the answers to these questions.

1. What caused Ellis to have a miscarriage?

2. How was another person hurt at the murder scene?

3. Who could have stopped Ellis' death sentence?

4. What is a free vote in Parliament?

5. How short can a 'life' sentence be in fact?

C Decide if the following statements are true or false.

1. Ellis did not intend to kill Blakely.

2. Ellis got sympathy because she was good-looking.

3. The jury had no trouble in deciding her guilt.

4. Murder rates fell in the 21st Century.

5. The Home Secretary cannot change sentences.

The Magdala Tavern, 2008 (closed 2016). Ellis shot Blakely outside this pub.
Wikimedia Commons. Photo by Mike Quinn.

Chapter 15

Margaret Thatcher: Prime Minister

Wikimedia Commons. Photo by Chris Collins of the Margaret Thatcher Foundation.

Margaret Thatcher (1925 – 2013)

Margaret Thatcher was born in 1925 in Grantham, Lincolnshire[①], where her father owned two grocery shops. She gained a degree in Chemistry at Somerville College, Oxford in 1947,
5 where she was President of the Conservative Association[②], showing her early interest in politics. She later qualified as a barrister[③].

She became a Member of Parliament[④] in 1959, for Finchley in London, a seat[⑤] she held until 1992. From the beginning
10 she was a believer in a small state, low tax government.

She was promoted quite rapidly, and became party leader in 1974. In 1979 the Conservative Party[⑥] won the election and Thatcher became Britain's first woman Prime Minister. She proved to be a strong and popular leader, winning two more
15 general elections[⑦]. Her free market policies permanently transformed the political landscape[⑧], controlling inflation, privatizing[⑨] many industries, limiting trade union power and bringing in flexible labour markets.

Her inflexible determination to bring in a flat tax[⑩] on all

---

① **Lincolnshire:** イングランド中東部の北海に面した州。
② **the Conservative Association:** 章末注を参照。
③ **barrister:** 章末注を参照。
④ **Member of Parliament:** イギリス議会の国会議員（MP）。
⑤ **seat:**「選挙区・議席」Finchley はロンドン北部の選挙区。
⑥ **the Conservative Party:**「保守党」
⑦ **general election(s):**「総選挙」
⑧ **political landscape:**「政界・政界のありよう」
⑨ **privatizing:**「民営化」
⑩ **a flat tax:**「均一の税金」一種の人頭税を実施した。

adults, and her increasingly negative attitude to the EU eventually destroyed her popularity. As a result, her own Party deposed[1] her in 1990. She moved to the House of Lords[2] in 1992, but generally had a quiet retirement. She died in 2013, and her ashes are buried at the Royal Hospital[3], London.

Her Importance

Margaret Thatcher was not the first British woman to be prominent in politics, but she helped to make it seem normal for a woman to be in charge. She did not promote women to top jobs, apparently preferring to be a queen bee, but today that is different. Theresa May became Prime Minister in 2016, and appointed women to be Home Secretary, Education Secretary, and Justice Secretary, among others[4], with eight women out of 23 Cabinet[5] members. 32% of MPs elected in 2017 were women, the highest ever. In 2017 the leader of the Scottish National Party[6] was also a woman, Nicola Sturgeon, leading to very public disagreements between her and May. It is notable that parties more publicly committed to gender equality, including Labour, have never had a woman leader.

Thatcher, along with American President Ronald Reagan, helped to bring in a new approach to politics. In Britain she broke the postwar consensus of a large welfare state. She believed that the state had no business owning large parts of the economy, and set about privatizing state-owned corporations, including coal, steel, gas, electricity, telecommunications and the railways. The results remain open to dispute. For example, the railways generally offer a much better service than before, and passenger numbers have more than doubled, but many rail companies now belong to foreign state-owned rail corporations, such as SNCF[7] and Deutsche Bahn[8], and the government is still subsidizing rail.

Thatcher also believed that trade unions had too much power. Certainly the 1970s saw a great many strikes in Britain that seriously damaged the economy. She brought in new laws to curb[9] that power, and such laws have continued to be passed since her time. Strikes are now a last resort[10]. More to the

---

[1] **depose:**「退ける」
[2] **the House of Lords:**「(イギリス議会の) 貴族院」イギリスは二院制となっており、このほかに選挙で選ばれる the House of Commons がある。
[3] **the Royal Hospital:** Thatcher は退役軍人のための病院 The Royal Hospital, Chelsea に葬られた。

[4] **among others:** P.47 注①参照
[5] **Cabinet:**「内閣」
[6] **the Scottish National Party:**「スコットランド国民党」

[7] **SNCF:** フランス国鉄。
[8] **Deutsche Bahn:** ドイツ鉄道。1994年に民営化されたが、株式は国の所有となっており、実質的には国有鉄道。
[9] **curb:**「抑える・抑制する」
[10] **resort:**「(頼るべき) 手段・方策」

point, trade unions are now regarded with suspicion by the majority of people, and union membership is low. The decline of traditional unionized[①] industries has helped this change.

She believed in home ownership, and sold off council houses[②] to the occupants. This was highly popular with the purchasers, but has led to a serious housing crisis now. Houses are too expensive for many people to buy, and renting privately is also expensive. There is a shortage of new houses, a shortage which corresponds closely to the lack of new social housing[③], housing that would have been built if it had been allowed.

Above all, Thatcher believed in a low tax, low spend approach. She thought that people should keep the money they earn and spend it as they choose, rather than have the government take it from them and spend it on their behalf. This policy certainly creates more freedom, but it equally certainly creates greater inequality, as the government is less able to redistribute income. But perhaps people should take personal responsibility for their lives.

Thatcher transformed the political landscape in Britain. The Labour Party won the 1997 general election, and held power for 13 years, but it could only do so by accepting many of Thatcher's reforms, including privatization and the restrictions on unions. Indeed, Thatcher saw Tony Blair[④] as her natural successor. After 2010 the Conservative government went further than Thatcher, privatizing the Royal Mail; Thatcher had refused to do so, rather sweetly, because the queen's head is on all postage stamps.

Perhaps her main influence has been to transform the Conservative Party from a generally pragmatic, unintellectual party into a highly ideological one. Many see the Conservatives as the party of opportunity – one could point to the transformation of London since the gloomy 1970s. Others see the Conservatives as the 'nasty party'[⑤], not caring about the devastation[⑥] of old manufacturing towns. It really depends on one's point of view.

[①] **unionized:**「労働組合の強い」

[②] **council house(s):**「公営住宅」

[③] **social housing:** 地方自治体等が供給する住宅。

[④] **Tony Blair:** 1953年エジンバラ生まれの労働党党首。1997年から2007年まで三期にわたり首相を務める。

[⑤] **'nasty party':** 2002年 Theresa May（2016年から二人目の女性の首相となる）は、保守党について人々が「卑劣な政党（nasty party）」と呼んでいるとして、保守党の危機を訴えた。

[⑥] **devastation:**「荒廃」

********** NOTES **********

the Conservative Association: 1924年に設立され保守主義を支持・研究する学生組織。オックスフォード大学ではＯＵＣＡ（オーカ）と略して呼ばれている。

barrister:「法廷弁護士」イギリスではこのほかに solicitor「事務弁護士」と呼ばれる法律家がいる。barrister は法廷での弁論などを行い、solicitor は法律文書の作成や法律相談などを担当する。

Questions

A Choose the best answer to the questions.

1. **How long was Thatcher Prime Minister?**
   - a five years
   - b eleven years
   - c thirteen years
   - d sixteen years

2. **Why did Thatcher stop being Prime Minister?**
   - a She retired.
   - b She lost a general election.
   - c She became ill.
   - d Her colleagues forced her to quit.

3. **What did Thatcher not privatize?**
   - a the railways
   - b the steel industry
   - c utilities
   - d the postal service

4. **What did Thatcher believe in?**
   - a high tax, high spend
   - b high tax, low spend
   - c low tax, high spend
   - d low tax, low spend

5. **What can we say about strikes?**
   - a They have remained rare.
   - b They have remained common.
   - c They have become rare.
   - d They have become common.

B Write the answers to these questions.

1. What two mistakes brought Thatcher down?

2. What is surprising about Labour Party policies after 1997?

3. What has been a problem of selling off council houses?

4. In whose name does the Royal Mail apparently operate?

5. How did Thatcher change the Conservative Party?

C Decide if the following statements are true or false.

1. Thatcher was both a scientist and a lawyer.

2. Thatcher left Parliament in 1992.

3. Thatcher did not give top jobs to women.

4. The railways still depend on the taxpayer.

5. Thatcher believed in personal freedom.

Margaret Thatcher's birthplace, Grantham, Lincolnshire.
Wikimedia Commons. Photo by Thorvaldsson

テキストの音声は、弊社 HP http://www.eihosha.co.jp/ の「テキスト音声ダウンロード」のバナーからダウンロードできます。

illustration：内山　弘隆

Iconic British Women from History
アイコニック・ウイメン：イギリス女性と現代社会

2019年1月15日　初　版
2022年2月10日　2　刷

著　者 © Simon Rosati
注解者 © 近　藤　久　雄
　　　 © 河　野　淳　子
発行者　　佐　々　木　　元

発 行 所　株式会社　英　宝　社
〒101-0032 東京都千代田区岩本町 2-7-7
☎ [03](5833)5870　Fax [03](5833)5872

ISBN 978-4-269-15022-5 C1082
印刷・製本：モリモト印刷株式会社

本書の一部または全部を、コピー、スキャン、デジタル化等での無断複写・複製は、著作権法上での例外を除き禁じられています。本書を代行業者等の第三者に依頼してのスキャンやデジタル化は、たとえ個人や家庭内での利用であっても著作権侵害となり、著作権法上一切認められておりません。